The Poetry Review

The Poetry Society, 22 Betterton Street, London WC2H 9BX

The Poetry Review

The Poetry Society, 22 Betterton Street, London WC2H 9BX
Tel: +44 (0)20 7420 9883 • Fax: +44 (0)20 7240 4818
Email: poetryreview@poetrysociety.org.uk
www.poetrysociety.org.uk

Editor: Maurice Riordan
Production: Michael Sims

ISBN: 978-1-900771-87-0 ISSN: 0032 2156
Cover illustration Sarah Hanson / Début Art

. . .

SUBMISSIONS

For details of our submission guidelines,
please visit the *The Poetry Review* section of
www.poetrysociety.org.uk

ADVERTISING

To advertise, visit poetrysociety.org.uk
or contact Robyn Donaldson on
+44 (0)20 7420 9886,
email: marketing@poetrysociety.org.uk

BOOKSHOP DISTRIBUTION

Central Books, 99 Wallis Road, London
E9 5LN, UK. Tel: 0845 458 9925
or visit www.centralbooks.com

PBS EXCLUSIVE BOOK SUPPLY SERVICE

Readers of *The Poetry Review* can receive many
of the books featured in the magazine post-free
by mail order from the Poetry Book Society.
To order, tel: +44 (0)20 7831 7468,
Mon-Fri, quoting *The Poetry Review*.

SUBSCRIPTIONS & SALES

UK individuals: £34 / Europe: £44
Rest of the World: £49
(all overseas delivery is by airmail)
Single issue: £8.95 plus postage.
Order from www.poetryreview.org.uk or contact
Paul McGrane on +44 (0)20 7420 9881.
Pay by cheque (sterling and US dollar
cheques only), credit card or Direct Debit.

The Poetry Review is also available on audio CD.

The Poetry Review is the magazine of the
Poetry Society and was first published in 1912.
A subscription to *The Poetry Review* is included as
part of membership of the Poetry Society. It is also
available from leading bookshops. Views expressed
in *The Poetry Review* are not necessarily those of
the Poetry Society; those of individual contributors
are not necessarily those of the Editor.

Charity Commission No. 303334

CONTENTS

Poems

Poems *from* Poetry

Prose

Reviews

National Poetry Competition 2014

EDITORIAL

One of the pleasures of editing this issue was to sift through the work published in *Poetry* over the past twelve months and choose poems for our annual exchange. I wasn't actively looking for the 'best'. I passed over poets who are already well known, or better known, to UK readers. Other than that, I followed my inclination, a current taste for what is agile and noisy, a wayward tendency perhaps to favour excess over restraint.

And now this selection sits beside the 'home' team of poets mainly, though not exclusively, from the UK. How do they compare? It turns out they have more in common than one might expect. Some of these poems could have been written either side of the Atlantic. This is hardly surprising with Eva Salzman, a poet who has a foot on each land mass. But I suspect Stephen Sandy's 'Modest Proposals', say, or Rosanna Warren's 'A Way', might equally have been written here.

On the other hand, the poems of Tommye Blount, Danez Smith, Natalie Diaz, and others, just couldn't. American poetry, on the basis of this sampling, has a mix of race, sexuality, violence, and an awareness of military involvement that we don't have. It also has an instinctive rapport with jazz and the movies that gives these poems an altogether different textural feel to what we know. There are, too, subtle differences in language, not just the occasional interjection, such as "The end end" or "Yeah, as if", but a more general propensity to individualise phrasing, to say it just 'the way I'm going to say it'.

This is not that poets here lack linguistic ambition, rather that it follows different pathways. Jacob Polley's hooded lyricism and Steve Ely's sounding of the word-hoard from the fourteenth-century Yorkshire mystic, Richard Rolle, suggest one tendency. Such poetry has a wildness that hearkens back through the ages to Anglo-Saxon and taps into the Northern mythos of the meres and the fastnesses.

Entirely by coincidence, two poets – Fran Lock and Simon Barraclough – use the model of Christopher Smart's 'My Cat Jeoffry' to produce their own modern creatures but do so under the franchise of a classic poem – albeit one that comes somewhere between the King James Bible and Walt Whitman. Such an approach is culturally more self-reflexive and resonant than the unfettered self-expression of a culture that remains, well into the new century, in the making.

But for all that, the poems speak to each other comfortably. The fact is the genius of the language resides less in its localised idioms and registers than in its syntactical flexibility. It's a rubbery beast with a voracious appetite for anything in its reach. Maybe it has to do with that King James Bible in every hotel-room drawer from Seattle to Boston, Lincs!

In any case, our tongues are more intertwined, more genetically variegated and virally contaminated with each other, than one might suppose. And in the higher manifestations of poetry, it is a shared tradition of invention, wit, and transcendent yearning that prevails. Or so it seems when passed, in one tiny sample, through the filter of yours truly.

Maurice Riordan

JONATHAN EDWARDS

Song

So come to me, by plane, by train, by car,
by unicycle, girl, by self-drive van,
by Twitter, FaceTime or by sleight-of-hand,
oh lease yourself a pack-mule, a giraffe,
oh steal yourself a moped, pay a man
to carry you here, girl, on piggyback,
or get the railway to lay extra track
up to my door, up to my waiting hands.

So come to me, on fresh air or on credit,
oh hoof it, leg it, go by Shanks's pony
over stony ground and live off grass
or hedgerow, girl, whatever you can forage,
and rest on river banks, beneath a roof
of forest. Navigate your way by stars
or GPS, but listen, girl, be quick.
Oh speed yourself towards my waiting skin.

So come to me. Oh score yourself a gun,
a false moustache, girl, and a native tongue,
and smuggle yourself in the early hours
under wire and across the border.
Or buy yourself a wrecked and promising
motorhome and let dawn find you, girl,
with oil-stained cheeks, just working till it purrs
or goes. Oh drive towards my waiting bones.

So come, by raft, by hovercraft, or do
a goose-fat, nose-clipped, brave or water-winged
breaststroke through the sea that's parting me
from you, or fit a tractor engine to

a li-lo, rubber ring, a rowing boat.
My home's made by these hands, this skin, these bones.
My home is made of straw and fragile stars.
Oh come to me. Oh make this where you are.

Gen

Look at them, coming round the corner,
bouncing, flouncing, boho
beehives, tattooed, corduroy-looned, sneakered
scumbags, skinheads, brogue-shod uni fools, or
look, they're me, they're you, but slightly
cooler, lust- and roll-up-fuelled, artfully
spectacled idea junkies, pushing,
selling, anyone of us could be
John Lennon, Jesus, coke and sneezes
forced through nostrils that are pinned
or pierced. Look, these feather-boa'd
vegans or these leopardskinned
animals, with their x-rated
bodies, their needs never sated
by hands-free friends or look, their palm-held
search engines, their razor'd heads turned
by beauty or a global crisis, these masters
of their own devices. For every word
they've #'d or abbreviated, each god
they've never worshipped, every song
they've downloaded, shook their arses to or sung,
I say bow down, bow down, the young, the young.

FRAN LOCK

Melpomene

And he says I have this hardly original
hole inside of me; that I am two things
infinitely: carnal and futile. He's right.
I am a bad wife, a wanting quarry
of witless worry; lank rage, grim schlock,
and stroppy poverty. I am sleazed in
the green of The Land, raining down
her birdsong in blows. The dubby
crush of my keening does his head in.
I sink kisses into screams like pushing
pennies into mud. And he says he is *done*.
From the wordy murk of my loss come
lanterns and daggers, and I am my country:
mean, gutless and Medieval; a dread
mess of battlements and spoils. He cannot
love me, grieved to my gills and grinding
exile like an axe. He cannot love me,
howling out my mutant blues to no one.
My semi-automatic sobbing wakes
the neighbours. I am sorry. I have tried
to live lightly, to live like *gadje* girls,
to make my mouth an obedient crock
of homage; to keep my swift hands soft
in illiterate peachiness. But I am from
an ugly world, an ugly world with ugly
songs for busking in an underpass. I am
not one of your machine-washable muses,
my face a cotton swab. I cannot come
clean, come cosy, come tame and fond.
His suckling fund of human love destroys
me. I am not good. I am a ferreting girl
who steals from shops, a perfidious febrile

girl who gobs off bridges; a hedging
and fretting girl, one eye on the exit.
I am terrible. I drink myself to a fly-
tipped farrago of falling down. No decorum
in me. My mourning is eloquent strumpetry,
and ruin porn will always be the whole
of my Law. I am sorry. And he says he
cannot love me in my insolent libidiny;
my shrill pandemic ditties: poems bleating
like woebegone ringtones. He cannot love me
in my words, raptures dragged from the slangy
waste of Norn. He says he will have none,
when a poem is a viral fire that spreads my anger
round; a typo-tastic war grave in which I bury
my dead. And he says I am *damaged*. I frisk
the heart for sadness, find it waiting
like a toothache. It is true. Thrice fool girl,
dangled at a day's end, what have I got
besides? There is only this particular fire
in me, this brief biotic craze of light, a halo
like a yellow enzyme: luciferase, fanatical,
and *dragging us down*, he says. He leaves
and slams the door. I breathe again. The TV
leaks a sour myrrh meaning evening. I scuff
my breath on the edges of an empty room.
Here is the moon, poor feme sole,
and the orange stars in their cold swoon.

And I will consider the yellow dog

And Smart saw God concentric in his cat.
Smart's cat, artificing faith from cyclone
volition. There is no God in you, yellow
dog. Your breath is our daily quicksand;
you juggle your legs into an avid heap.
You are bent on death. There is no God
in you. You are imperfect and critterly.
I *will* consider you, for all of that. Today,
as you joust farewell to the park; the pack
in their garrison palsy, tails agog, and you,
cocking your head to cup Madam's strewn
bark, your nose like an antique brooch
in the sun. I will consider you, yellow dog,
as you twist in a rapt mechanical dream.
I will consider your coat, the colour
of fenced gold; how you are your own
secular halo. I will consider your skull,
the narrow skull of a young gazelle
whose victory is leaping. And I will
consider your eyes, their hazel light
a gulp of fire, those firewater eyes,
holding now a numb depth down,
and milkier flickering monthly. I will
consider your youth, when we didn't
know if you would saunter or quake;
when we didn't know if you
would prove savvy or giddy or both.
It was both. Our frank amaze at your hardy
smarts! Our silly delight at each degree
of more-than-human knowing. I will
consider you, yellow dog, your pale
moods and your gazing; your fidgets

and your snoozes. There is no God in you,
the deep-time of a dog year is enough.
And lately you are wiser than all zero.
Dear dog, creaking like a haunted house,
I will consider you, from bucking *young
'un* to patient as settling porter; how you
held the pack when Fat Man was small
and a zoomy nuisance of wriggling. I will
consider your narrow self, aslant against
my chest in grief, in grieving, overwhelmed,
when you were the busy broom that swept
the pieces of me together. Yes, I will
consider the yellow dog, his bestowing
snout in the chill a.m.; his royal cheek
and his dances. A yellow dog comes only
once and is hisself: brilliant, final and entire.

DAVID SERGEANT

Air strike
See all those people standing down there?

O what a remarkable world we live in!
Where people can go up into dust
just like that, raindrop impact
on every molecule:
                              waiters
throwing their dishes into the air
and running out of the restaurant
into the televised square
of your sight, yelling as they go –
arms, heads, legs, O fat
blisters of bubblewrap
popped
            just like that –

or fireworks bursting asunder, poor fuel
too soon used up.

Like finding a –
                    finding a –
well, like finding a –
                              cup

holding just one slug of honeyed nectar

when everything you'd heard had led you to expect,
everything you'd learnt had led you to prospect
on the expect
                  ation of flowing litres
                              of honeyed nectar.

How easy it is to make a ghost, to be haunted!
And what a remarkable world we live in!

Where any segment might burst
at any moment
                  you'd presume
into dust, the child behind its father
                                      outside my window
calling
        on the pavement
                    which tuggles
beneath their feet
             into fragments,
                      heads, legs, meat, O
all heading off
             in every direction,
chunks of wedding cake torn by hungry paws.

O little one caught
In the magniloquent impact
Of indiscriminate creation!
               or something like that –

boiling water poured
into a nest of ants on a cruise to Timbuktu, out of a clear blue
sky
     thatched little villages
                    coming apart
snakes of impact
           writhing
               little darts
of tinsel dropped from the tree

of life, oh, you might begin to suspect
if you're anything like me
that this magic
              annihilate unlock
                        lurks
at the back
        of your sight,
it might unleash on anything!

Enough to drive you mad, I'd say.

Imagine your wife, your kids:
                    little firecrack
lurks at the elbow joints – turn to look
and pop! every pixel
             on their faces
is writhing to change its channel.

Enough to drive you mad

            I'd say.

The white
cloth on the breakfast table
              tremors
like heated milk
beneath your hands, it is perched on the boil.

You can't look up.
Your eyes have learnt to kill.

Shaking your superflux
Never, never, never, never, never

So in this yacht
there is not a lot

wrong, each patented faucet
cost $40,000
and blends seamlessly
into the silver thread

which runs through every room,
into and out of the catacomb

of lamé beds and silver-seeming cushions
sewn together by teenage lamas
and specifically designed for nookie:
a cruder man than me might term it
The Shagging Parlour.

It's hidden behind the helicopter sheds
and the guestroom lined with white stingray hides.

An intruder would have nowhere to hide,
such is the impressive preponderance of glass and mirrors.

Beyoncé once sang for a rumoured $2,000,000
at a party hosted by the son of desert tyrant torturer and *at time
        of writing* international persona non grata Colonel
        Gaddafi.
But let us not judge, it would be wrong.
I hereby declare that I will personally sing
at the birthday or bar mitzvah or bigamous wedding
of a dictator of *your* choice

for $2,000,000
which is one million two hundred and twenty seven thousand
       nine hundred and nine pounds and fourteen pence
at time of writing.
After all, it's only a voice!
Anywhere, anything:
sing, sing, sing, sing, sing.

You might point out that this is dross
and you'd be right
         but then
my shambling bear of an auditor
a lot of the world is dross
and look at me, I'm only mimicking.
Don't chase me from the stage.
Don't eat me in a rage.
I'm just part of the welter of print on the printed
       and unprinted page.

EVA SALZMAN

Vermont Still, Life

I was afraid
of a dark barn perched on the meadow incline
behind the old house with no electricity
he dropped me off at,

of its dark, its hollow mouth,
a lumbering primitive
on stilts

the hue of russet carbonised,
leaning

where foliage consumed the view, all amoral. Trees
stepped steeply up as we'd just done
towards the summer's museum.

He showed me the well for the taste
of iron ice

then left. The books had kept each other company
the many years they didn't need us.
Of numerous confusing rooms one dwelled in the one

only, under the dim duet of gas lamps
or in a flashlight's private corridor of beam.

Days dragged, slowed by shadow and the faucet drip's
cellar cove, bedrooms swallowing wedding rings
until the peace grew wilful

and the half-wrecked porch seemed fortunate
in vanishing, wrongly placed

because backwards facing. There, where spiders spun
and hung, and chipmunks darted like sparks,
I waited for the dusk with wine

as the acclimatising animal I am,
browsed stillness

and watched a wall of tightly coiled branch
and trunk,
straitjacket vines, that living case.

Alone a week, amazingly, my pulse still beat,
day chasing nightmares

built on higher slopes of a duller dulling house with phones
and all conveniences as if to redress
the standard dream's striptease of civilities.
When the rain came thundering

I stepped out naked to wash my hair,
slipped into the cold shoes
of puddled twisted blades of grass,

was lightning rod
on a wild hill with a tangled heart.

Animal Couplets
for Juliette

Why do dogs have paws instead of claws
and cats have claws in addition to their paws?

Why muzzle a muzzle? Aren't dogs' cold, wet snouts
the snuffling heart and soul of what a dog's about?

Well, skip the question of doggie pants and woofs.
Horses don't have paws or claws, but hoofs.

Most birds go chirp and tweet. Are standard 'beaks'
just lower-class, while 'bills' are the height of chic?

Men and women often lose their heads of hair.
Unfair. Beasts have lots of fur to spare.

Although most can boast of hefty overcoats
ducks have ones which make them bob and float.

Whiskers surely come in handy in the wild
yet only ornament a grown man's smile.

Why have four legs when two will often do?
God over-legged some puddings ere he was through.

After millipedes he seemed to get less keen
so the spider's eight seems pretty mean.

GRETA STODDART

Letter from Sido

So, my very dear mother, speak on the verge of death, speak in the name of your inflexible standards, in the name of the unique virtue that you called 'true elegance of behaviour' – Colette

I'm writing this by the light of a barn
in flames, Madame Moreau's. One wonders,
with the old man gone and her gout getting worse.
I see the poor rats running all over the garden.
How beautiful it all is!
I saw old Loeuvrier go by last week
in his coffin. I do like watching funerals,
one can always learn from them.
But don't ever let me see you in mourning for me,
you know how I loathe black – what's wrong with pink?
I've been making a big bed-jacket from an old pink quilt.
I want to be buried in it. Thank you for your invitation.
No, Josephine is *not* sleeping in the house.
I sleep here alone, so please, no more fuss.
No more stories of wicked tramps kicking down the door.
Give me a dog if you like.
Ever since your father died I cannot bear
another human being in the house at night.
Dear child, you write that you're not well,
is it the city, the air too thick and sour?
Do you remember that time I went to the Curé
in a fury about something only to dance home
with that beautiful pelargonium cutting he gave me?
This time he gave me a cactus – it's here on the sill.
Beyond it I can see the blaze dying down.
I keep waking up. The other morning at three
I watched a very handsome garden spider slowly
descend and drink from my blue bowl then draw
herself, heavy with chocolate, back up to the ceiling.

Et voilà! a new companion.
I've been going through the books on your father's shelves.
It's such a bore – all the love in them.
In real life, my poor Minet-Chéri, folk have better things to do.
I hear from your brothers – so you write about your life?
You see? I warned you about going to confession,
I always said it led a child to play around too much
with words, make things up, navel-gaze.
Better to hold your tongue – punish yourself yourself.
This cactus is very rare. It's pink.
The Curé says it's about to come out.
As I write, a stray is winding her way round my ankles.
She looks quite blue in the glow. I'll cook her an egg.
I did the same for poor Yvette's girl the other day.
I don't do it because I'm good, heaven knows.
I do what'll set my mind at rest – you know me.
The other day I found a caterpillar hibernating,
a bird had pecked out her stomach.
I have her healing now in a little matchbox of sand
on my bedside table – what a beauty she'll be
and all the more so for having suffered!
There's just black sky now where the barn was.
You know the worst thing about being old?
– the sight of my hand on the sheet.
I still play chess with my little wool-seller.
Your father would have been delighted,
the dead are a peaceful company, my child.
The Curé tells me this cactus only flowers once
every four years. And I am dying.
You will forgive me, won't you, Minet-Chéri,
you will understand that I can't come to you.
You who took three days and three nights to leave my body.
Children like you are the most beloved because
they've lain so high, so close to the mother's heart.

I can hear my pen scratching in the dark.
I have grown very thin.
When I'm at the water pump in the morning
I feel my dress touch the backs of my legs,
the sun is just warm and I feel ten years old.
How can I leave now?
How could I leave that thing to flower alone?
Someone needs to see it into the world.
I want it to be me peering into its closed pink heart.
I want to watch it push its slow suddenness
out and quiver there in the warm air.

PAULA BOHINCE

Christmas Day

We woke late, lonely
for food's hypnosis, the mindlessness
of a prix fixe: duck confit,
skin like gift wrap;

haricots verts, devil-may-care
as strewn Army men;
escargots in divots, snug as children
in boarding-school beds.

Waters fetched, still
and sparkling, imbue a wavery
soft-lit mood. Burgundy is poured,
obvious as blood

from mortal wounds.
Silver murmurs to itself
in French, in this the oldest café
in Paris. Voltaire's desk

proffers the argument of mind
v. flesh at the head of a stair.
We don't look where
the lamb one party over

smells too real, of grass
and sacrifice. White cloths
suffuse the air with starch. We cough,
suddenly aged, ill.

Here comes our waiter bearing
every cake and éclair.
A wick twists a black serpent up
to the (*forgive us*) chandelier.

First Snow

Reclined in cerulean panty, alone, but filled
with guilty, adolescent laughter. When the designs
arrive, as shredded lace, they become
the ripped white sundress, buttons bulleting
every wall, O he climbed the escape, with his Summer
teeth, giving a story to the bed. The body
worshipped then pleases now itself, recalls
the bride doll kept in the childhood house, grime-
stiffened satin, lashes that lifted
when she was taken from the *B*-engraved cradle.
The crucial fall, snow signaling temptation relaxed into
action, pulse points cooling under its spell,
the certainty of ice, the sweetness of any virgin.

ANNIE FREUD

Bujold

She marries him in a 'marriage blanc'
so that he can stay in the country.
He is a fugitive whose visa has run out
and there is every kind of impediment:

the ambitious local cop in dark glasses
and leather jacket, determined to hound them,
the provocative younger sister, the absurd mother
giving a huge white wedding nobody wants.

An explosion of debauchery, revelry and waste
saw the church lose its hold on the medieval world,
she tells her class of docile undergraduates,
and feels the need for a full-time man.

At forty, she is ravishing in a haggard way
and he looks seedy with his too-long hair.
There are some good jokes about lonely, frightened
people trapped in forced proximity.

I know this place is a mess, but don't touch anything.
I know where everything is. The cafetière is complicated.
Love prevails in the end. We never see them
in bed and they only ever kiss at the wedding.

SUSAN WICKS

Birdsong

Thinking that somewhere there is still this
rich disharmony of chirp and twitter-
flutter, sparrow, thrush and finch
and blackbird, cadenced signature
of ring-dove cooing on a falling breath
to distant cock-crow, other creatures
scratching their distinctive sounds on waking –
is waking to find yourself years younger
in a place where silence grows to chatter,
adults talking softly underneath you,
moving about in rooms, performing gentle
ordinary tasks – refilling kettles,
slicing bread and turning on the gas,
cracking an egg into a crusted pan.
Then stairs become a shadow-staircase down
into a kitchen, out towards a garden
where already runner beans are twisting
scarlet-flowered upwards full of bees, and lilac
hangs its many heads and weeps, and light
is fingering the path, the fence, the rails
that hum already with the almost-
now-arriving first train of the morning.

JACOB POLLEY

Elfred

He went into the marshes, a few
with him. I was one. Winter.
We scavenged wood. It smouldered.
Ate eels from the dark we had to
break into with axes, birds we envied
as we snapped their necks.
Shapes in the smoke and worse

in the mist. Reed beds. Reed walls.
We drank from the dark
in that great unhallowed
hall of reeds. Fear? Everywhere. That this
place was no place, but an ingrowing
of the mind. His. And we

figments of it. He was Heron, narrowed
at the murk's edge. Staring
at what? We couldn't see. Whoever
asked, shall we do this, shall we
do that, he stared through. I caught it,
counting beads in the frilled black

floors of ice. Treasure-
struck by the glasswork, inlaid
with gold leaves. Days I dreamed
with my eyes open, knowing
nothing's true worth. He led us
deeper. Of each he asked a riddle, one
he'd never heard. We knew he'd heard
them all. 'Then you must make

like the night,' he said, 'which smiths
silently to trick out every reed-
tip and dripping rockface with fine
light-fastenings of frost.' Light-
fastenings. We liked that. Fell

further into ourselves.
Isolate murmurings. Hours binding
our breath into basket-traps. Not
speaking. By the slow putting-out

of my blade by rust I knew
my turn neared. No man so far
had tried him twice. He was Pike,
rising from the depths

of likelihood to say what in one
gulp. I woke, my beard pointed
silver. Solder of ice on the shit-
pit where I strained to line up
the parts of my little device. *I am...*
Again. *I am...* Began over
and over, *I am, I am.* And over and
over, I couldn't remember. Holes

where words had been. My wit
fallen through. What skill I'd thought
I had, to wire song to sense and so
intricate a slyness fit

to confound my king, had melted.
Went to him anyhow, a mere
man in a hovel of damp wood-smoke
on an island at the mist's heart.
Crouched in under

the sweating lintel. Stood blinking
back the gloom. He was griddling
flatbreads on a hiss of furred
embers. He said my name. Worried
the heat with a stick. Waited.
Who am I, I said. My voice cracked.
Who am I that is led without

leadership into this waste?
My king was wise. I followed him.

Now he sits, gut-sick on eel-meat,
supposing his kingdom will one day
come, like an almsman lugging
a sackful of heads, to say he was
right all along and begging to tender
to him crown, coin and borough.

To draw about him then his cloak
of reeds and turn his back will please
my king more than sunrise, more than
the dark he poled in his childhood,
which has afforded him again a
stronghold of slime. Say who I am

who sees himself an old man
beside the sea, writing in black
water all these words, just to get to
this reek of flatbreads blackening.

STEVE ELY

Hugo of Fyselake

Therfor thei token Jeremye, and castiden
hym doun in to the lake of Elchie, [...]
wherynne was no watir, but fen; therfor
Jeremye yede doun in to the filthe. (Jeremye, XXXVIII: 6)

Followed the football, fell.
Face-down black muck,
sucked black water:
askr, flittermouse, tade.

Hole in Cuthbert's earth,
a small one: Mamma pumping
his chest and shrieking
to Mary, wiping off worms.

The undertaker's rule: two cubits,
a candle for Richard. Lauds,
the light extinguished –
her dead boy quacking like a duck.

The White Hart

Robertus Swynherd, of Elmsall-on-the-Hill,
smote Butcher's taxman on high road
twixt Pomfret and Danum.
Broadcast groats for stubblefield gleaners.

And fled his gret-headed gazehounds
to Lindholme's asylum, with Roben,
Iohannes and Alan of Barnysdale;
where they feasted on pikes and venison.

And flushed from birch scrub, a hart
of fifteen hands, bull-burly,
fathomed in tines, breasting Torne-spate
to Wood House and Hatfield beyond.

At Stane-Ford on Dun, Robert's
gret-headed gazehounds did him grapple
to ground; where *Grip* he skull-spiked,
divers tossed, and hobbled.

He forded to Fyselake and galloped
the ingas through Kirkhouse to Moss,
where Robert, with Roben and Willelmus
called *Red*, corralled him to Fenwick's mire.

Where houndis assailed him, and they let loose
arrows; but broadhead-pierced and ripped
of flesh, he leapt from Went's watter-world
and brok beyond Askern, to Campsall on-the-stone.

On wold his ailing legs found strength,
ran horse and hounds ovr oppen field
to Wrang-brook, Upton, Elmsall-on-the-Hill;
where he frothed blood, and fell.

Exhaust on *street* twixt Pomfret
and Danum, the houndys held him at bay;
whereupon the Swynherd strode
through the melee, and slew him by sword.

In the White Hart that night was meat
and much drinking, Robertus and Roben,
Willelmus called *Red*; in their cups throwing silver
in rushes for children; where also they slept.

And woke to the point of Butcher's sword,
were dragged in chains to Pomfret;
where Robertus and Roben, Willelmus
called *Red*, were strung up on Beastfair gibbet.

For they took the King's coin and meat
from his chace and laid about his servants
with staves: the eve of St. Leonard.
Wild-men came to Wentbridge by boat.

Iohannes and Hrothgar, Alan of Barnsdale;
many men of England. Across Hardwick moor
to Carleton, through Friar wood
to Beastfair; and cut them from the crows.

And laid them in their parish
at Ladychurch at Kirkby. Where Swein
and Arketil held carucates for geld,
and the turned plow runs with blood.

Eofor

Red bracken and leaf-litter
white thighs splay
beneath boarish buttocks
wrist-throats pinned
glimpsed snatch of fox-fur   vixen
squealing pigeons skyward

comes roaring from the brake
the hook-toothed god
of the bristling pizzle
rearing erect and spurting anemones
goring the gaffer
and lording   his lady
humped quivering in the loam.

Poems are taken from Incendium Amoris *('The Fire of Love'), a work-in-progress inspired by the life and writings of the mystic Richard Rolle (1300?-1349)*

SIMON BARRACLOUGH

from *Sunspots*

For I will consider my Star Sol.

For I am the servant of this Living God and daily serve her.

For at the first glance of the glory of God in the East I worship in my way.

For this is done by fixing espresso and watching the pinkening light on
The Shard.

For then she waves her warmth across the scene and lifts the hearts of
those who took a Night Bus at 4 a.m. to clean HQs.

For she tickles the orbitals of foxes in their stride and hies them home.

For having risen and settled into her groove she begins to consider herself.

For this she performs in eleven degrees.

For first she does the Planck to strengthen core stability.

For secondly she runs a malware scan for comets closing in.

For thirdly she completes the paperwork for eclipses total, annular and
partial.

For fourthly: flares.

For fifthly she sorts her sunspots into pairs.

For sixthly she gives neutrinos Priority Boarding.

For seventhly she referees the arm-wrestling match between the upstart
fusion and gravity.

For eighthly she weaves flux ropes and thinks up skipping games.

For ninthly she degausses her plasma screens.

For tenthly she is profligate with her photons.

For eleventhly: star jumps.

For having considered herself she will consider her neighbours.

For she runs a cloth around the ecliptic to make it gleam.

For she oils the wheels of any planets gliding there.

For she sends invites out to wallflowers in the Oort cloud.

For she issues shadows for children to dodge as they make their way to
school.

For she shakes out her blankets for devotees of helioseismology.

For when she takes her prey she plays with it to give it a chance.

For one planet in nine escapes by her dallying.

For in her morning orisons she loves the Earth and the Earth loves her.

For she is of the tribe of Tyger! Tyger!

For she hands out colouring books to chameleons in the morning.

For when it is time to rise she blushes to be seen at so intimate an hour.

For when it is time to set she is crimson ashamed to run out on us.

For though she neither rises nor sets she thinks it best that we believe so, so
    that we can take our rest and fuel our waking with anticipation.

For she lifts oceans over mountains without thinking.

For she tries to solve the puzzle of the weather, placing *this* here and *that*
    there and attempts to even out the air.

For she is a mixture of gravity and waggery.

For she's a stickler for solstices.

For she booms like a woofer for those that can hear.

For she cares not what lives as long as all live.

For she takes her time.

For she lenses the light from distant stars to swerve it into our sockets.

For sometimes in the winter haze she's as pale as a lemon drop and lets us
    watch her bathe unpunished.

For she never calls in sick.

For her colours are open-source.

For every raindrop's an excuse for Mardi Gras,

For she will work on her drafts for a million years and release them typo-free.

For she will lash out and then regret the hurt.

For she promises radio hams jam tomorrow.

For your power grid is a cobweb she walks into when she steps off her porch.

For she kept mum through the Maunder Minimum.

For her behaviour is definitely 'on the spectrum'.

For she keeps dark about dark matter but she definitely knows something.

For she plays Miss Prism in *The Importance of Being Furnaced*.

For she offers board and lodging to Turner's 'Angel in the Sun'.

For she made a great figure in Egypt for her signal services.

For she can fuse the wounded parts of a broken heart and release the
    lost mass as hope.

For she spins plates to create auroras.

For she leaves clues all over the place: some cryptic, some quick, some general knowledge-based.

For she is hands-off.

For she tends to micro-manage.

For she lays down squares of light for your pets to sleep in.

For she turns a blind eye to all the creeping, swooping killers of the night but leaves a Moon-faced night-light on.

For her sunquakes flatten no buildings, gridlock no cities, disgorge no refugees.

For she is not too proud to dry your smalls.

For she gives us heliopause and time to rethink disastrous decisions.

For Ray-Bans.

For she polarises opinion.

For her secrets are waiting to free us.

For she appreciates Stonehenge and visits every day.

For she sets herself by the grid of Manhattan.

For she will kill you with the loving of you.

For she can shine.

Poems from *Poetry*

TOMMYE BLOUNT

The Bug

lands on my pretty man's forearm. Harmless,
it isn't deadly at all; makes his muscle flutter
– the one that gets his hand to hold mine, or
ball into a fist, or handle a gun. It's a ladybug,
or an Asian lady beetle everyone mistakes
for a ladybug – eating whatever
it lands on. My pretty man is asleep – at ease, or
plotting like the bug. Or maybe the bug
is a blowfly – eating my pretty man's tan
from his pretty arm. My man swats it
without waking, as if he's dreaming of an enemy,
or me. When my pretty man isn't asleep
he's got a temper.

           No, he is not
asleep. He's wide awake and wants me to tell you
I'm wrong. Blowflies don't eat skin,
they lay eggs on skin. He knows all about
blowfly larvae. Napoleon used them
to clean war wounds, my cold pretty man
says in that pretty way,
with his cold pretty mouth. He's eaten plenty
of bugs before. On night watch,
over there. Over there, they're everywhere.

TRACI BRIMHALL

Better to Marry Than to Burn

Home, then, where the past was.
Then, where cold pastorals repeated
their entreaties, where a portrait of Christ
hung in every bedroom. Then was a different
country in a different climate in a time when
souls were won and lost in prairie tents. It was.
It was. Then it was a dream. I had no will there.
Then the new continent and the new wife
and the new language for no, for unsaved,
for communion on credit. Then the daughter
who should've been mine, and the hour a shadow
outgrew its body. She was all of my failures,
my sermon on the tender comforts of hatred
in the shape of a girl. Then the knowledge
of God like an apple in the mouth. I faced
my temptation. I touched its breasts with
as much restraint as my need allowed,
and I woke with its left hand traced again
and again on my chest like a cave wall
disfigured by right-handed gods who tried
to escape the stone. It was holy. It was fading.
My ring, then, on my finger like an ambush,
as alive as fire. Then the trees offered me a city
in the shape of a word followed by a word
followed by a blue madonna swinging from
the branches. A choir filed out of the jungle
singing hallelujah like a victory march and it was.

GABRIELLE CALVOCORESSI

Captain Lovell,

Shakey Eyes Horton had nystagmus too.
That's what my father said and took me
to the record store so we could buy him
and take him home to listen. Babe says
he's so square but we go all over. We listen
to music for hours and dance around
the house like crazy skeletons: loose

with all our bones knocking, we go,
"click click click" and wave our arms
and shake until we rattle all the china
in mom's cabinet. He turns the volume
up and we spin like planets round the sun.
Babe says he's no fun but I know different
because I see him laughing and I *try,*

which she just never does. She walks
into the house with Jasper waiting in the car.
She grabs some clothes or asks for money,
though she doesn't even come to do that
anymore. They don't even talk. Last time
we had the music on loud and we were dancing.
I was letting my head swing back and forth

and she just stood and watched us with the strangest
look and I said, "I'm Shakey Eyes! Come dance,"
and moved my arms around. I followed her up
the stairs, swinging like a satellite and going,
"Ooh ooh oooooohhhhh," just like a low-down goodfor-
nothing so and so. I know she thinks I'm funny
but she didn't laugh and I said, "Come *dance!*

You know you've got the blues." Then I said, "You're
no fun." She said, "You don't know him like I do."

NATALIE DIAZ

It Was the Animals

Today my brother brought over a piece of the ark
wrapped in a white plastic grocery bag.

He set the bag on my dining table, unknotted it,
peeled it away, revealing a foot-long fracture of wood.
He took a step back and gestured toward it
with his arms and open palms –

> *It's the ark,* he said.
> *You mean Noah's ark?* I asked.
> *What other ark is there?* he answered.

> *Read the inscription,* he told me,
> *it tells what's going to happen at the end.*
> *What end?* I wanted to know.
> He laughed, *What do you mean, "what end"?*
> *The end end.*

Then he lifted it out. The plastic bag rattled.
His fingers were silkened by pipe blisters.
He held the jagged piece of wood so gently.
I had forgotten my brother could be gentle.

He set it on the table the way people on television
set things when they're afraid those things might blow up
or go off – he set it right next to my empty coffee cup.

It was no ark –
it was the broken end of a picture frame
with a floral design carved into its surface.

He put his head in his hands –

I shouldn't show you this –
God, why did I show her this?
It's ancient – O, God,
this is so old.

Fine, I gave in, Where did you get it?
The girl, he said. O, the girl.
What girl? I asked.
You'll wish you never knew, he told me.

I watched him drag his wrecked fingers
over the chipped flower-work of the wood –

You should read it. But, O, you can't take it –
no matter how many books you've read.

He was wrong. I could take the ark.
I could even take his marvelously fucked fingers.
The way they almost glittered.

It was the animals – the animals I could not take –

they came up the walkway into my house,
cracked the doorframe with their hooves and hips,
marched past me, into my kitchen, into my brother,

tails snaking across my feet before disappearing
like retracting vacuum cords into the hollows
of my brother's clavicles, tusks scraping the walls,

reaching out for him – wildebeests, pigs,
the oryxes with their black matching horns,
javelinas, jaguars, pumas, raptors. The ocelots
with their mathematical faces. So many kinds of goat.

So many kinds of creature.

I wanted to follow them, to get to the bottom of it,
but my brother stopped me –

> *This is serious,* he said.
> *You have to understand.*
> *It can save you.*

So I sat down, with my brother wrecked open like that,
and two-by-two the fantastical beasts
parading him. I sat, as the water fell against my ankles,
built itself up around me, filled my coffee cup
before floating it away from the table.

My brother – teeming with shadows –
a hull of bones, lit only by tooth and tusk,
lifting his ark high in the air.

KNAR GAVIN

The Track Racer
for Marshall "Major" Taylor

A hoot is a hilarious person. Perhaps train
scream or owl, jeer. Often done by mouth.
A man may widen owl wide and give one away.
Hoots may result in bans, as in, "the crowd 'hooted'
the track star clean out of the sport."
Sometimes a hoot may be kept and saved
for later. For instance, "They didn't give a hoot."
A woman may sharpen a hoot
in the toolshed with the bread knives. So there
may be a toolshed, and this may be where the knives are kept
and the hoots. They come from chambers –
come at you with those wings. So when waiting in the toolshed hoot runs its owl talon over the knives. Else
it comes at you, other it stares.

·

In 1890, George "Little Chocolate" Dixon put his
foot on the world and held it there, waiting for the Major
to come. These were the days when extra layers
of name were glazed on – a way of saying both more
and less and not at all. In the case of the two-term moniker,
permit either/or – you may grab from the bag "Little". In France,
Marshall "Major" Taylor was *le Nègre Volant* –
you may grab from the bag "Flying".

·

Sometimes it's a bad investment to self-publish
autobiography – *what a hoot*. As in, pauperism
may wait for you with its long needles
readying to blow you out. Under the pauper's empty ton
a man gets baby-bird gaping with hunger. The Major

puts his wings inside and dies in Cook County Hospital
where it's too late. Hoot given, hoot held back. Ice-white nurses
come warm in their linens to fold back the wings beside
themselves, like any good cook come to shut a mouth.

This case of hoot has called for leg and wing and swoop.
Rise up, Major. Ghost-man old Birdie Munger's bike
– take back the front, it's time to owl.

TERRANCE HAYES

How to Draw a Perfect Circle

I can imitate the spheres of the model's body, her head,
Her mouth, the chin she rests at the bend of her elbow
But nothing tells me how to make the pupils spiral

From her gaze. Everything the eye sees enters a circle,
The world is connected to a circle: breath spools from the nostrils
And any love to be open becomes an O. The shape inside the circle

Is a circle, the egg fallen outside the nest the serpent circles
Rests in the serpent's gaze the way my gaze rests on the model.
In a blind contour drawing the eye tracks the subject

Without observing what the hand is doing. Everything is connected
By a line curling and canceling itself like the shape of a snake
Swallowing its own decadent tail or a mind that means to destroy itself,

A man circling a railway underpass before attacking a policeman.
To draw the model's nipples I have to let myself be carried away.
I love all the parts of the body. There are as many curves

As there are jewels of matrimony, as many whirls as there are teeth
In the mouth of the future: the mute pearls a bride wears to her wedding,
The sleeping ovaries like the heads of riders bunched in a tunnel.

The doors of the subway car imitate an O opening and closing,
In the blood the O spirals its helix of defects, genetic shadows,
But there are no instructions for identifying loved ones who go crazy.

When one morning a black man stabs a black transit cop in the face
And the cop, bleeding from his eye, kills the assailant, no one traveling
To the subway sees it quickly enough to make a camera-phone witness.

The scene must be carried on the tongue, it must be carried
On the news into the future where it will distract the eyes working
Lines into paper. This is what blind contour drawing conjures in me.

At the center of God looms an O, the devil believes justice is shaped
Like a zero, a militant helmet or war drum, a fist or gun barrel,
A barrel of ruined eggs or skulls. To lift anything from a field

The lifter bends like a broken O. The weight of the body
Lowered into a hole can make anyone say *Oh*: the onlookers,
The mother, the brothers and sisters. Omen begins with an O.

When I looked into my past I saw the boy I had not seen in years
Do a standing backflip so daring the onlookers called him crazy.
I did not see a moon as white as an onion but I saw a paper plate

Upon which the boy held a plastic knife and sopping meat.
An assailant is a man with history. His mother struggles
To cut an onion preparing a meal to be served after the funeral.

The onion is the best symbol of the O. Sliced, a volatile gas stings
The slicer's eyes like a punishment clouding them until they see
What someone trapped beneath a lid of water sees:

A soft-edged world, a blur of blooms holding a coffin afloat.
The onion is pungent, its scent infects the air with sadness,
All the pallbearers smell it. The mourners watch each other,

They watch the pastor's ambivalence, they wait for the doors to open,
They wait for the appearance of the wounded one-eyed victim
And his advocates, strangers who do not consider the assailant's funeral

Appeasement. Before that day the officer had never fired his gun
In the line of duty. He was chatting with a cabdriver
Beneath the tracks when my cousin circled him holding a knife.

The wound caused no brain damage though his eyeball was severed.
I am not sure how a man with no eye weeps. In the *Odyssey*
Pink water descends the Cyclops's cratered face after Odysseus

Drives a burning log into it. Anyone could do it. Anyone could
Begin the day with his eyes and end it blind or deceased,
Anyone could lose his mind or his vision. When I go crazy

I am afraid I will walk the streets naked, I am afraid I will shout
Every fucked up thing that troubles or enchants me, I will try to murder
Or make love to everybody before the police handcuff or murder me.

Though the bullet exits a perfect hole it does not leave perfect holes
In the body. A wound is a cell and portal. Without it the blood runs
With no outlet. It is possible to draw handcuffs using loops

Shaped like the symbol for infinity, from the Latin *infinitas*
Meaning *unboundedness*. The way you get to anything
Is context. In a blind contour it is not possible to give your subject

A disconnected gaze. Separated from the hand the artist's eye
Begins its own journey. It could have been the same for the Cyclops,
A giant whose gouged eye socket was so large a whole onion

Could fit into it. Separated from the body the eye begins
Its own journey. The world comes full circle: the hours, the harvests.
When the part of the body that holds the soul is finally decomposed

It becomes a circle, a hole that holds everything: blemish, cell,
Womb, parts of the body no one can see. I watched the model
Pull a button loose on her jeans and step out of them

As one might out of a hole in a blue valley, a sea. I found myself
In the dark, I found myself entering her body like a delicate shell
Or soft pill, like this curved thumb of mine against her lips.

You must look without looking to make the perfect circle.
The line, the mind must be a blind continuous liquid
Until the drawing is complete.

DOROTHEA LASKY

The End

Promising myself I would not do this again
Is what kept me going

A friend told me to
And I listened

Taking a thing to the end of its life
Is what I was made to do

I think I am not attuned
To the things that breathe

Well that's not true
I am in tune to breath and life

And little falls of flowers

When the moon was high
I went out to the stream

And brought in the water
For my folks, my kin, my brethren

I brought in the greenish milk
To feed the ones who were already dying

Oh did they go
Oh I do not know

SARAH LINDSAY

Attack Underground
Themiscyra, 72 BC

While Lucullus raided cherry orchards,
he left us to besiege,
grudgingly, this outlander fortress,
named for an Amazon queen,
while thinking of food and home.
Not one of us has seen
a single horse-borne warrior woman.
Meanwhile, we dug a tomb.

We intended it as the tunnel
through which we'd claim the fort.
We shored up the sifting roof
and dug by lamps
that shed more shadows than light.
At last we formed up underground
to attack with sword and fire,
but the enemy tossed in hives,

and in a cloud of stinging bees
our torches jerked and swung or fell
so we could hardly tell
where to strike, or what, for next
our enemy sent weasels in, and foxes,
which seemed to be done in jest
until we felt their teeth
and heard, more than saw, the larger beasts.

A wolf began my death.
I lay in men's and weasels' blood
and heard the body
that dropped at my side
ask, *What barbarian thought to make*
of thoughtless creatures weapons of war?
But a flung torch showed me the face
of a bear that said nothing, and died.
Then came the boar.

CLAUDIA RANKINE

from *Citizen*

When the stranger asks, Why do you care? you just stand there staring at him. He has just referred to the boisterous teenagers in Starbucks as niggers. Hey, I am standing right here, you responded, not necessarily expecting him to turn to you.

He is holding the lidded paper cup in one hand and a small paper bag in the other. They are just being kids. Come on, no need to get all KKK on them, you say.

Now there you go, he responds.

The people around you have turned away from their screens. The teenagers are on pause. There I go? you ask, feeling irritation begin to rain down. Yes, and something about hearing yourself repeating this stranger's accusation in a voice usually reserved for your partner makes you smile.

/

A man knocked over her son in the subway. You feel your own body wince. He's okay, but the son of a bitch kept walking. She says she grabbed the stranger's arm and told him to apologize: I told him to look at the boy and apologize. And yes, you want it to stop, you want the black child pushed to the ground to be seen, to be helped to his feet and be brushed off, not brushed off by the person that did not see him, has never seen him, has perhaps never seen anyone who is not a reflection of himself.

The beautiful thing is that a group of men began to stand behind me like a fleet of bodyguards, she says, like newly found uncles and brothers.

/

The new therapist specializes in trauma counseling. You have only ever spoken on the phone. Her house has a side gate that leads to a back entrance she uses for patients. You walk down a path bordered on both sides with deer grass and rosemary to the gate, which turns out to be locked.

At the front door the bell is a small round disc that you press firmly. When the door finally opens, the woman standing there yells, at the top of her lungs, Get away from my house. What are you doing in my yard?

It's as if a wounded Doberman pinscher or a German shepherd has gained the power of speech. And though you back up a few steps, you manage to tell her you have an appointment. You have an appointment? she spits back. Then she pauses. Everything pauses. Oh, she says, followed by, oh, yes, that's right. I am sorry.

I am so sorry, so, so sorry.

Citizen is published by Penguin on 2 July 2015. © Claudia Rankine, 2015.

STEPHEN SANDY

Modest Proposals

A longish poem about wallpaper.
A short lyric about discouragement in white.
A medium-length thesis of uncertain importance.
Another sonnet, about scholarship.
A couplet of olives.

A long narrative about the exaggeration of your absence.
Several quatrains about candle stubs.
That old sestina on Isaiah.
Palindromes about Scots presbyters of the 18th century.
Some rock lyrics from Benares.

A nature poem about committees.
Seven heroic couplets about Art Murphy.
Several more heroic couplets on Murphy's Law.
A ballad about studying Latin in Latium.
A masque for Mercedes and her Benz.

SOLMAZ SHARIF

Vulnerability Study

your face turning from mine
to keep from cumming

8 strawberries in a wet blue bowl

baba holding his pants
up at the checkpoint

a newlywed securing her updo
with grenade pins

a wall cleared of nails
for the ghosts to walk through

TOM SLEIGH

The Animals in the Zoo Don't Seem Worried

Looking at the lion behind the plate glass
I wasn't sure what I was looking at: a lion, OK,
but he seemed to come apart, not literally

I mean, but I couldn't see him whole:
Mane. Teeth. The slung belly pumping
as he panted and began to roar. His balls

sheathed in fur swaying a little. His tail's tuft
jerking in an arc like an old-time pump handle
rusted in midair. Somebody or something

I read once said that when Jesus had his vision
of what his father, God, would do to him,
that Jesus could only see pieces of a cross,

pieces of a body appearing through flashes
of sun, as if the body in his vision
was hands looking for feet, a head for a torso,

everything come unmagnetized from the soul:
the lion caught me in his stare not at
or through me but fixated on the great chain

of being that Jesus couldn't see and that
a zebra might gallop in – black and white stripes
marking longitudes of this world turning

to meat, bloody meat – this vision of an inmate
that Jesus's father helped to orchestrate by
making a cageless cage with glass instead

of bars – though the lion didn't seem to care,
he was roaring for his keepers to bring
him food, so everything's what it should be

if you're a lion. Nor did the sea lion
seem concerned about having gone a little
crazy, barking incessantly so I could see

the plush, hot pink insides of its throat,
though like the lion through the glass
there's this distortion, my reflection

I'm looking through that makes me float above
the zoo: and now this silence at closing time
pours like a waterfall in different zones

of silences that, pouring through my head,
surround roaring, barking, human muttering –
is any of that what being sounds like?

Or is it just animal gasping like what
Jesus must have heard from the thieves
hanging beside him, one damned, one saved?

What was in his heart when his vision
clarified and he saw it was a hand he
recognized that the nail was driving through?

DANEZ SMITH

Dinosaurs in the Hood

Let's make a movie called *Dinosaurs in the Hood*.
Jurassic Park meets *Friday* meets *The Pursuit of Happyness*.
There should be a scene where a little black boy is playing
with a toy dinosaur on the bus, then looks out the window
& sees the T. Rex, because there has to be a T. Rex.

Don't let Tarantino direct this. In his version, the boy plays
with a gun, the metaphor: black boys toy with their own lives,
the foreshadow to his end, the spitting image of his father.
Fuck that, the kid has a plastic Brontosaurus or Triceratops
& this is his proof of magic or God or Santa. I want a scene

where a cop car gets pooped on by a pterodactyl, a scene
where the corner store turns into a battleground. Don't let
the Wayans brothers in this movie. I don't want any racist shit
about Asian people or overused Latino stereotypes.
This movie is about a neighborhood of royal folks –

children of slaves & immigrants & addicts & exiles – saving their town
from real-ass dinosaurs. I don't want some cheesy yet progressive
Hmong sexy hot dude hero with a funny yet strong commanding
black girl buddy-cop film. This is not a vehicle for Will Smith
& Sofia Vergara. I want grandmas on the front porch taking out raptors

with guns they hid in walls & under mattresses. I want those little spitty,
screamy dinosaurs. I want Cicely Tyson to make a speech, maybe two.
I want Viola Davis to save the city in the last scene with a black fist afro pick
through the last dinosaur's long, cold-blood neck. But this can't be
a black movie. This can't be a black movie. This movie can't be dismissed

because of its cast or its audience. This movie can't be a metaphor
for black people & extinction. This movie can't be about race.
This movie can't be about black pain or cause black people pain.
This movie can't be about a long history of having a long history with hurt.
This movie can't be about race. Nobody can say nigga in this movie

who can't say it to my face in public. No chicken jokes in this movie.
No bullets in the heroes. & no one kills the black boy. & no one kills
the black boy. & no one kills the black boy. Besides, the only reason
I want to make this is for that first scene anyway: the little black boy
on the bus with a toy dinosaur, his eyes wide & endless

        his dreams possible, pulsing, & right there.

ROSANNA WARREN

A Way

The whole trick of this thing ... is to get out of your own light.
  – Marianne Faithfull

She said she sang very close to the mike
to change the space. And I changed the space
by striding down the Boulevard Raspail at dusk in tight jeans
until an Algerian engineer plucked the pen from my back pocket.
As if you're inside my head and you're hearing the song from in there.
He came from the desert, I came
from green suburbs. We understood
nothing of one another over glasses of metallic red wine.
I was playing Girl. He played
Man. Several plots were afoot, all
misfiring. One had to do with my skimpy black shirt
and light hair, his broad shoulders and hunger
after months on an oil rig. Another
was untranslatable. Apollinaire
burned his fingers on June's smoldering lyre
but I had lost my pen. The engineer
read only construction manuals. His room
was dim and narrow and no,
the story didn't slide that way though there are many ways
to throw oneself away.
One singer did it by living by a broken wall
until she shredded her voice but still she offered each song,
she said, like an Appalachian artifact.
Like trash along the riverbank chafing at the quay
plastic bottles a torn shirt fractured dolls
through which the current chortles an intimate tune.

DEAN YOUNG

Romanticism 101

Then I realized I hadn't secured the boat.
Then I realized my friend had lied to me.
Then I realized my dog was gone
no matter how much I called in the rain.
All was change.
Then I realized I was surrounded by aliens
disguised as orthodontists having a convention
at the hotel breakfast bar.
Then I could see into the life of things,
that systems seek only to reproduce
the conditions of their own reproduction.
If I had to pick between shadows
and essences, I'd pick shadows.
They're better dancers.
They always sing their telegrams.
Their old gods do not die.
Then I realized the very futility was salvation
in this greeny entanglement of breaths.
Yeah, as if.
Then I realized even when you catch the mechanism,
the trick still works.
Then I came to in Texas
and realized rockabilly would never go away.
Then I realized I'd been drugged.
We were all chasing nothing
which left no choice but to intensify the chase.
I came to handcuffed and gagged.
I came to intubated and packed in some kind of foam.
This too is how ash moves through water.
And all this time the side doors unlocked.
Then I realized repetition could be an ending.
Then I realized repetition could be an ending.

POETS READING

> An occasional series in which poets write about their
> current reading

. . .

Emily Berry on Kristin Prevallet's book of mourning

"Kristin Prevallet writes about mourning as if I might desire that state." I read this in a blog post about the American poet Kristin Prevallet's *I, Afterlife: Essay in Mourning Time*, a book I have become enamoured of. A friend recommended it to me last year when I was looking for things to read on the subject of mourning, partly to elucidate my own long and delayed experience of it, partly for academic reasons, if the two can be separated. This book, which Prevallet describes in the acknowledgements as "a gathering together of poems and essays", made me understand something I knew on some level but had not managed to articulate: that mourning is a kind of desire. And this understanding was important to me.

Of course, the psychoanalysts have much to say on this point, so it's not a new idea, but since when did anybody have a 'new idea'? Sometimes you read a book at the right time and that was the case with this one; it helped to illuminate some things I was in the dark about – I mean it picked out certain details of the darkness. As Prevallet writes: "Through the words that are in me I tried to decipher the night, and then remembered that darkness has its own resolution." When she says "resolution" here I think of how we use the word to talk about high-quality images, and there is a more specific definition from which this use emerges, where "resolution" means: "the smallest interval measurable by a telescope or other scientific instrument; *the resolving power*". Prevallet wrote the various texts that make up *I, Afterlife* over several years following her father's death by suicide. In being a book about mourning it is also a book about distances, the distances that we cannot traverse, even if they are ever so small ("the smallest interval"). For Prevallet the act of writing is a means of negotiating with these distances: "This gesture of approach is the closest you will get to the other side."

The book's trans-genre nature (besides poems and essays, it also includes visual images, a "preface" and a transcript of the eulogy Prevallet read at her father's funeral) is an aspect of its "resolving power", an admission and even a celebration of the way things remain, despite our efforts, in pieces. Disjointed, fragmentary, but whole, the book's form embodies the idea that there is no "tidy package that presents a simple truth" of consolation for the bereaved; rather, comfort comes from "rewriting the script that assumes that spaces have to be filled in". She writes, "I have to live with my losses as one would live without an arm: being constantly aware of the phantom limb sensation that wants so desperately to connect, to be filled in, with flesh."

In *I, Afterlife*, to live with loss is also to live with want. I'm remembering lines from 'Meditation at Lagunitas', Robert Hass's great poem about a more general kind of loss: "Longing, we say, because desire is full / of endless distances". *I, Afterlife* is preoccupied with this notion, with spaces, gaps and holes, and their "energies, force fields, and pulls". The book's epigraph – an excerpt from Alice Notley's 'At Night the States', a poem of mourning for her husband, Ted Berrigan – lures the reader into this force field with its own strangely seductive lament: "At night the states / whoever you love that's who you / love / the difference between chaos and / star I believe..."

That Prevallet manages to convey or even transfer this state to the reader, as Laura Hinton (whose blog I quote above) suggests, may be due to the work's combination of directness and elusiveness, whereby the speaker's mourning/wanting is always at a slight remove, never entirely graspable, just as loss is never graspable: "I may refuse to reveal the truth of what I am mourning"; "beware of being absorbed by an essay that is grieving, because you will lose your place and be eradicated"; "Have I warned you not to fall in love with a girl who refuses to let go of grieving?" Her ambivalence reminds the reader that, actually, mourning is not a state to be desired, even though she insists, "Desire plays an important role in this essay." She calls her text "essay" even at moments when it is formally closer to poetry. It's worth noting, as Hinton comments, that 'essay' comes from the French *essayer*, to attempt. *I, Afterlife* resists, even denies, the possibility of closure ("The text that is grieving has no thesis; only speculations... Nothing is closure"); like desire itself, it is process, rather than product.

If this is a book about the slow reconciliation of an individual to a state of unrequited love, what Freud called "the work of mourning", it is also (of course) about the desire for a language to facilitate this process, for a means of coping with the fact that "the lack of communication between the living and the dead makes the living wild with fear". Prevallet's language is a "gesture of approach", which acknowledges how far she still remains from "The means of arriving through and around the facts of longing", but this is the nature of mourning. "Distance must remain distance", Freud wrote in a letter bearing the news of his daughter Sophie's death. "Believing that holes can be filled with language is dangerous— only space itself occupies empty spaces", Prevallet says, but *I, Afterlife* is not about the so-called inability of language to 'express the inexpressible'. Actually, it is a celebration of the way that language – poetry – in its mess and precariousness, with its own immanent distances ("There is nothing certain about language, just as there is nothing certain about where a person goes after he has disappeared"), manages to find its way through "incommunicable terrain". And what it communicates is, of course, very hard to communicate. The psychoanalyst Donald Winnicott said: "At the centre of each person there is an incommunicado element, and this is sacred and most worthy of preservation"; *I, Afterlife* preserves this element, that place where all our wants and our losses converge. "In doubting the possibility of a tidy afterlife," Prevallet writes, "I have come to compose a fragmented system of believing. I call this poetry."

I, Afterlife: Essay in Mourning Time *(New York: Essay Press, 2007).*

OMPHALOS

I would begin with the Greek word, omphalos, meaning the navel, and hence the stone that marked the centre of the world, and repeat it, omphalos, omphalos, omphalos, until its blunt and falling music becomes the music of someone pumping water at the pump outside our back door.
– Seamus Heaney, 'Mossbawn'

> *An occasional series in which poets write about a place*
> *central to their imaginative world*

. . .

Pascale Petit

When I say the word *omphalos* I find myself in the Fauverie at the Jardin des Plantes zoo. If my *omphalos* has a *genius loci* it's one of its residents, the black jaguar Aramis. This big-cat house is where I started to write my second collection, *The Zoo Father*, and later on my sixth, *Fauverie*. It was where I found a way to write about my father and the terrible things he had done, through animals I love, and to imagine him, and try to redeem him, as my favourite place on earth: the Amazon:

He seems to have sucked
the whole Amazon
into his being, the storm-

clouds of rosettes
through a bronze dusk.
I've been there, sheltered

under the buttress
of a giant, felt
the air around me –

its muscles tense,
stalking me
as I stumbled

through dense fur [...]

('Black Jaguar at Twilight')

It's an odd location to call my *omphalos*, but "all paths lead to the Fauverie" where I "dined with the *tigre* / in his den". It's where I chat to the animals and to my father's ghost. I can't return to his flat as someone else rents it now. I did try once, but the woman who answered my timid knock wouldn't let me in. The Fauverie was where I recovered after disturbing visits to him, and where somehow he merged in my mind with a powerful predator.

The felines spend the day in the outside enclosures of this octagonal Art Deco house. Inside is their night quarters where they are fed at the end of alternate days in a public ritual. This spectacle begins with the wheeling out of the trolley, laid out with white rabbits, turkeys and horse meat, the switching on of lights in the corridor behind the cages, and the opening of each upper hatch to lure them indoors. It's enthralling to watch them pounce down with a thud, one by one, on to the lower floor. The caracal Black Ears is let in first, then the ferocious North China leopards, followed by Aramis (when he was lodged there), the snow leopards and clouded leopards. Since Aramis moved to the renovated zoo at Vincennes last spring, I also have to go there, to see him with his new mate, Simara. But even without him the Fauverie keeps drawing me back.

I go to the Fauverie at feeding time, just as I visited my father at lunchtime over the two years I knew him. The first day I met him I was late and he was starving. He served lunch even before we had a chance for us to get acquainted and this would form the pattern for our meetings –

each was a prolonged meal. He was suffering from emphysema and could barely speak, as he needed all his energy to breathe, so I did most of the talking. I had recently travelled in the Venezuelan Amazon and told him about that. Somehow the two places merged in my mind – his cluttered dingy room became my shadowy Lost World.

In Venezuela's remote highland, with its flat-topped mountains or tepuis rising out of the jungle mist, is the world's highest waterfall, Angel Falls. The falls plunge down a sheer amphitheatre of rose quartz sandstone set deep in a canyon of Auyán-tepui, and I suspect that the Fauverie reminds me of this amphitheatre. Angel Falls is so high that it's silent, as most of the water evaporates before it reaches the ground from its kilometre-high drop. But there is a roar from the lower falls in Churun River. When I camped at the base, storm clouds obscured the head of the falls and the swollen lower cataracts shook the ground. At dawn the howler monkeys added their otherworldly bellows. One night, I heard the gruff cough of a jaguar. So there is this trio of roars in my memory: the silent falls with their rumbling sub-falls, the howlers, and the jaguar who woke me up as I lay in my hammock.

That ethereal, hostile place felt like home. The mountaintop is haunted by the evil spirits of the local Pemón tribe, but I still sometimes dream about being up on the summit, of discovering a school in the meadows among the criss-cross of rock columns. The Paris of my childhood is there, along with the mawari – the spirits the Pemón fear so much they won't step on the surface. I'd had recurring dreams of my father living up there, just before he contacted me. He had vanished from my life for thirty-five years and all I had were some dark memories of him when I was a child in Paris. Until he summoned me, my father was mythic as a mawari demon. Even after I met him, he remained unreal, and he died before I could get used to the shock of his reappearance.

There were many enchanting Amazonian species in the Ménagerie when he was alive, including king vultures, macaws, toucans, coatis, sloths, pumas, and two jaguars, Pataud the black male, and Bébelle the gold female. The big-cat house, then and now, is like a navel around which the zoo sprawls, and around that, the city of my birth, with its star-formation boulevards and city gates.

Jacob Polley

Here's my childhood with its tumbledown barn in whose clay walls are embedded old bottles and bits of old bottles, with its cobwebby lofts and empty animal sheds. Tattie Pot Lonning runs behind these sheds, between our yard and the back field, until it comes to a cement floor on which the cows cross the lonning to and fro, from the milking parlour to the byre and the field. When they have to cross, the farmer scrapes around red gates to make a corridor for them, but the cement floor is always caked in cow shit, either slithery-wet or cooked by the sun into a vegetal mask that crisps up like seaweed and begins to lift at the edges. Cross the cement and there's a T-junction, with Tattie Pot Lonning terminating in another lonning, which runs left a short distance to the main road and right into further lonnings that spider-vein the fields and pastureland behind the village.

In summer, these lonnings are fine dust that's churned up in clouds every time a tractor roars through, only to settle again on the hedgerows and nettle leaves. In autumn and winter, and often in spring and summer, the lonnings are mud, deep enough in places to suck my boots off my feet: two steep-sided chevron-printed ruts, ground in by the tractors' huge rear wheels, are divided by a central island of firmer mud, straggled with grass. Unlike the dust, which is pale grey, the mud is dark, sometimes the numb dark of the knocked-off TV, sometimes the sticky brown of a malt loaf. In winter the lonnings freeze: the chevrons are baked hard and dusted with frost and every hollow and dip is sealed with a lid like brittled milk.

I scuff down the main lonning, between hedgerows set with five-bar gates that open into fields – the Pond Field, the Fallen-Down-House Field – and soon come to a fork. I branch right into the less-used lonning, whose hedgerows – un-passed-between by tractors and trailers that would keep them knocked back – arch into and over the lane. Here the ruts are full of deep grass, and the ditch between the hedgerow and the lonning's cow-parsleyed edge is wilder with nettles, brambles and rearing foxgloves. This lonning leads steeply down towards the Solway Marsh, and in winter the pools that collect in its lower landings are often frozen into long alleys of frictionless, grass-green ice, electric for sliding on. The mossy-wet wooden gate at its end is being closed over by hedgerow and copse. But I take a left just before this glooming-in, under the ghost-grey columns of beech trees, and wade along another lane of grass and nettles that eventually rejoins the main lonning at the gate to the Mink Field.

I find them first in the garden, little bones, little jaws crumbed with earth. I scrape them clean. Then I start to search for them, soon learning the likely places: in the woodpile, in hedgerows, old nests, dark corners, and in the fresh dirt at the entrances to the burrows in the Mink Field, named for the day Sarnie and I saw quick-slung creatures slinking in and out of the sandy holes in the bank and decided they had to be, not stoats, but mink escaped from a mink farm. On a trestle table in the barn I arrange the bones in puzzles.

Sarnie lives down the other end of the village with his mum, dad and two sisters. His older sister, Molly, has straight black hair and a face of ivory, a skirt sewn with tiny mirrors. Sarnie himself is a year or two older than me. He's shown me how to tie a slipknot and we've set snares around the fields, deploying the loops where rabbits had scuffed low archways through the hedges, and rigged nightlines in the pool down North End, under the Green Bridge. Sarnie's bedroom is a narrow room under the eaves at the front of his house, as mine is under the eaves at the front of mine. There he shows me a box of blown eggs, the freckled shells bedded in tissue paper like polished stones, weightless when he lets me lift one between my thumb and forefinger. There's an air of illegality around these eggs, an intimation that they've been stolen from nests, that they must remain as secret in their lidded box as they should have remained in their high trees.

Beyond the farmland, where all the lonnings run out, is the Solway Marsh. Though cattle graze the unfenced marshland, this place feels vacant, exposed, trackless. Or it's me who feels vacant, exposed and lost in it. Out here, the quality of sound is different, too. Tiny noises are carried miles on the air: geese honking from above, cattle lowing from below, traffic-rumble from across the Firth in Scotland, and the wind blowing across the mouths of cattle-grids, burrows and sinkholes, so the very earth seems to drone.

Is it any wonder I have trouble getting myself home when I'm supposed to? "You could have been lying dead in a ditch," Mum says. She's telling me off for being late. She's grounding me.

That night I'm woken last thing when Dad fits the crank to the bolt on the right-hand side of the stove and cranks the bolt up and down to rattle the ash and dead cinders through the grate and into the ash-pan. When he opens the doors of the stove to feed it, I hear the red heat rush. He shakes on coal from a coal hod, the rim of the hod rhythmically bashing the door-edge, then shuts the doors, boxing away the rushing in the stove's iron belly. The immersion heater lives in a small cupboard at the top of the stairs to my bedroom. It rumbles and hisses like thunder and rain. My bedroom is anciently raftered and these oak rafters tick and creak, remembering the wind. The house breathes and thinks. There's not much traffic through our village and the silence is hoarded, as if in a great shell. Late on, someone walks under my window, each footstep ringing like a bright new metal. Because there's no distance in the dark, when the barn owl hoots it could be fields away or just behind the curtains, on the other side of the glass, stooped on my windowsill, white as a bone.

Essay

AFTERSONGS

Amali Rodrigo on medieval graffiti poems from Sri Lanka

> *To have your soul lanced*
> *by her loveliness*
> *is like offering your own head*
> *to a mahout's jewelled hook*

A UNESCO World Heritage Site, Sigiriya (or Lion Rock) in north-western Sri Lanka is home to some of the world's oldest examples of ekphrastic poetry. It is chronicled in the *Cūḷavaṃsa* as a royal pleasure palace and fortress built by King Kashyapa in the fifth century CE. The palace was constructed on the summit of a 200-metre high sheer-sided rock, surrounded by terraced water gardens on the plains below, and was possibly an attempt at recreating an earthly paradise similar to the mystical city of Alakamanda, a city of gods among the clouds ruled by Kuvera, the god of wealth. The western flank of the rock is believed to have been decorated with approximately five hundred frescoes of 'cloud maidens', twenty of which still remain.

Kashyapa, the son of a non-royal consort, seized the throne through patricide, walling his father alive into the bund of a reservoir. The strong defensive position of the palace was in anticipation of retaliatory war by his brother and rightful heir. When the battle finally took place, the desertion of Kashyapa's armies led to his suicide. Sigiriya was then abandoned. Later, it was converted to a Buddhist monastery and again abandoned, though it remained alive in local legend as a place of mystery and wonder, and for centuries drew visitors from many parts of the country.

Placed below the frescoes is the highly polished 'mirror wall' where these visitors inscribed *kurutu gee*, or 'song-poems', that were immediate, personal, and often sensual. The poems respond to the frescoes, the place, and also to previously inscribed graffiti, forming an uninterrupted ekphrastic dialogue that spans four centuries as the majority of these inscriptions date from the eighth to the twelfth centuries.

Sigiriya was rediscovered during British rule, when an army major happened across it on a horseback journey. The inscriptions came to the attention of archaeologists and historians only in the late 1800s. The identities of the women depicted in the frescoes have been fiercely debated ever since; they have been viewed as princesses, queens and members of the royal court, ladies of the harem or *apsaras* (heavenly nymphs) or representations of the goddess Tara.

Nearly 1,500 complete song-poems or poetic fragments have been deciphered to date. The poems often take the form of couplets and quatrains and occasionally contain prose addenda. The language is medieval Sinhalese, or Eḷu, a more erudite register (that does not admit Sanskrit tatsamas, or loan-words and is restricted to use in poetry). It is an unstressed language and poetic meters are based on syllabic instants (mātrās), and not heavy/light syllables. Although ten metrical systems have been identified, Yāgi (42 mātrās in the scheme of 9:11//11:11, each poetic line consisting of two metrical lines) is by far the commonest. It is a meter that falls easily into speech rhythms of the language, much like iambic in English. These meters can be divided broadly into unrhymed couplets, end-rhymed quatrains or a combination of the two. Internal rhyme in all cases is optional.

It is interesting to note that the rhythm of two lines in identical meters need not correspond. What is required, however, is that the pause for breath occurs on the same syllable or mora. Thus this engenders an infinite variety of rhythms. Epigraphist Paranavitana notes that poets were also often musicians, picking out the rhythm on a drum or lute before supplying the words to it, and the more popular of such verses may have crystalised into meters.

Considering their genesis, it is hardly surprising that not all the

Fresco, Sigiriya, Sri Lanka. Photo: © Hiranya Malwatta, 2015

deciphered verses have poetic merit. Some also remain fragments, not because of weathering, but because the writer gave up, unable to satisfactorily complete a metaphorical thought. But a notable element of the graffiti poems is the conscious effort taken by many writers to conform to then-current aesthetic standards of verse, demonstrating a familiarity with poetic conventions. This is remarkable as only two writers have explicitly identified themselves as poets. Many were from diverse backgrounds and occupations, such as a bookkeeper, a drummer, Buddhist clergy, members of royal households, an ironworker, a physician, a superintendent of the slaves. Only a handful of verses are by women.

One song-poem aims the following criticism at verses that limit themselves to describing "things as they are seen":

Description alone
makes not a poem
but an empty vessel

In classical Sanskrit aesthetics, it is the quality of *rasa* that gives rise to aesthetic pleasure in any form of art, hence the essence of poetry. It is defined as "[when] a feeling, emotion or a mental state, which by nature is of a fleeting character becomes more or less enduring". The word *rasa* occurs several times in the graffiti, referring to it being embodied in poetry, paintings and speech. It is also engendered in the mind of the gazer when encountering a beautiful object. Such persons are "sensitive" and "cultivated" and are *sa-hrdayas* or "those with a heart".

In Paranavitana's critical evaluation of the graffiti, he identifies several kinds of *rasa* contained within the poems: *adbhuta-rasa* (sentiment of wonder, here connected with place), *srngara-rasa* (erotic sentiment, including aspects of love in union and separation), *karuna-rasa* (lament), *hasya-rasa* (humour and wit) and *santa-rasa* (tranquillity). The latter is of particular interest in the way it interacts with Buddhist metaphysics, giving rise to epigrammatic and philosophical verse on the one hand, and on the other, verse that is highly didactic, advising on the dangers of sensual attachment to women.

One of the many poetic devices used to communicate *rasa* is compression. Although a poetic line consisting of around twenty syllables may seem like a long line in English, it is in fact extremely compact in this syllable-heavy language.

Fresco, Sigiriya, Sri Lanka. Photo: © Neranjana Gunetilleke, 2015

It does come as a surprise to find multiple similes and metaphors working within the narrow compass, gesturing towards several interpretations. For instance, in one poem, the comparison of the women's blue eyes gives way to the eyes of a deer and then to the light of crystal lamps. However, these are not simple cataloguing but a compounding of passing time with the changes in perception – from the initial moment of encounter, to the memory of it on the way back, and finally the mind altering the perceived and the remembered images, influenced by changes in the physical landscape (now it's night, and the moon has risen):

Blue eyes come to me again like deer
at dusk, climbing down the cliff past moonrise
their borrowed light is that of crystal lamps.

The nature of the mind and an intricate tracing of the stream of consciousness are a common subject matter among the graffiti and reflect the influence of Buddhist philosophical thought. Furthermore, there is little etymological distinction between the words denoting 'heart' and 'mind', and they are often used interchangeably, giving rise to an interesting ambiguity in many of the poems.

The use of stock conceits and floral symbolism, too, contribute to the enhancement of suggestive power. A woman's breasts are often likened to swans, and a beautiful face, male or female, to the moon. Flowers have multiple uses, both secular and religious. They were offered in worship as well as in welcoming a guest, or used as personal ornamentation. The lotus is a symbol of purity, linked to the metaphorical image of it growing in mud, but with the flower rising clear out of the mire. The blue lotus, or the *nil mahanel*, in particular, appears frequently in literature and Buddhist myth as an auspicious sign. Some poems subvert this by likening the flower to the skin of a darker-complexioned woman, where dark skin is not considered alluring.

Ambiguity, allusion, simile, metaphor and irony are examples of indirect or "crooked speech" that were devices necessary to handle the compressed couplet form.

There is also one "message poem", obviously an imitation of Kālidāsa's Meghadūta (cloud messenger). This poem is a precursor to an entire canon of long poems, such as the Hansa Sandeshaya (Swan Song) that was to develop a few centuries later, first in imitation of Kālidāsa, and gradually developing their own indigenous formal properties:

O cloud, sail to my beloved whose heart
is spent, whose lips are parched
and tongue is thirsting. O tell
her how she must take faith's refuge

There are several strands of dialogue running through the song-poems: a writer addressing the women represented in the frescoes and their response or talk amongst themselves; poems addressing fellow travellers; poems that respond to verses encountered on the mirror wall, and so on. The device of dialogue or *uba-bas-lakara* is not recognised in classical Sanskrit poetics and is believed to be an indigenous development at the time. *Ubabas* in relation to ekphrasis, giving voice to silent works of art as a poetic device, wasn't to develop until many centuries later in world literature:

She said *touch my waist* and I did!

You are a boor my friend to put such words
in a lady's mouth!

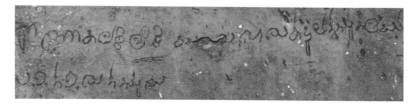

Graffiti poems on the 'mirror wall'. Photo: © Amali Rodrigo, 2015

The translations are based on the transcriptions made by Senarat Paranavitana, Sigiri Graffiti, Vol 2 (Oxford: OUP, 1956).

O the enchantment of breasts
like swans, tipsy
on the nectar of lotuses

> She drew me to a nook
> with the promise of a touch
> made a thief of me –
> and you too a man ever slinking
> through rear doors!

Girl, isn't it enough that you quarry
our secrets, must you stiffen
us too with longing ?

> How long she stares, tear-glazed,
> down this rough road
> fucked again and again in men's minds
> this is all she'll ever know of love

As a fleeing deer may pause
to turn towards its fear –
in the vast thicket of her grief
she smiles

> Love her yet wound her deep
> O forgive me gentle one
> the cuckoo too cries upon the hill

O the magnificence of heaven's
nymphs lazing on this knoll –
can a man be blamed for the hand
that leapt to unhook a girdle?

Midway through the climb, fulfilment looming, how blind I was
to the great suffering
that stood beside my desire

Dawn breeze
the scent
of lotuses

In the mansion of an awakened mind
hearing is a door. Guard it with diligence.
O how my whole being quakes
at the deluge of a woman's smile

– Novice monk

The man whose lust is rewarded
by this gold-skinned girl – isn't he as one who, having warmed
himself by the fire, lays down his head in it?

As an areca tree flourishing near water
may yet set roots further afield
O faithless ones, you'd live in a ruin
though a mansion's near

–Buddhist friar

She's half turned away
though her eyes hold mine,
a small pink hand stealing
up to widen her robe

Heavens have unleashed
a lashing rain. Wind-ripped buds
gather deep upon the earth.
The sky is red with swarming
fireflies, the curlew's lonesome
call rings the falling night – Oh love
what use are such missives
in your forever-absence?

O haughty one, why do you dodge
behind the screen of rock
when a real woman's here?
                              – A woman

You are as dew
on a lotus petal.
Knowing this, men are drawn,
then bewildered
at its loss
              –Buddhist friar

The fair woman taking
a sapu bud in her hand
bent my mind like a stalk

Overheard:
  Looking up at these women
  my eyes are pulled to the peak

The man unmoved by beauty is no poet
but a stringed puppet!
                   –*Poet Mihindal*

                Art lays bare the nature
                         of consciousness;
                a stand of curling hair – and the infinite
                    stirring the mind
                                –*Buddhist friar*

        The women on the massif
        emit lightning's brilliance –
        how does the painter endure
        his great affliction?

                Behind the sweep of yak-tail fans
                a jewel-flicker of eyes –
                yet I too am a woman prettified
                by gold necklaces
                            – *A woman*

The figure of the woman is excellently
                        sketched;
this hand, this eye so alive. Yet no one
can give them utterance

You brag about your classy verses
pilfered from another's thoughts –
when the golden peacock steps out to dance
the black sparrow, too, reels on the grass!

Ah the cuckolded king
is pacing hither and thither –
while his women linger
smiling on the rock!

Gold-skinned women undoing their hair
throw coquettish glances at passing men.
I alone noticed the charm of the dark one

I am Sela Boyi, I wrote these two verses:

A flower revealed a woman's mind,
and a god-king's trodden by a mere man.
Such loveliness is all mine to reign!

Ah you think much of yourself my man
as a bull shoots loose when the harness slips
supposing he too can clap and dance!
                    – *Wife of Sela Boyi*

Eons on this rock
knowing a desirable man
shall never come

THE THREE AGES OF MULDOON

Paul Muldoon, One Thousand Things Worth Knowing
Faber, £14.99, ISBN 9780571316045

reviewed by Ben Wilkinson

. . .

Back when *The Poetry Review* used to include caricatures, Paul Muldoon emerged from its pages as a rattlesnake. Sporting his trademark Dylan-esque barnet and NHS specs, his trickster's tie wriggled from a hieroglyph-inscribed basket. The image sticks because it fits. For the past forty years Muldoon has danced to his own tune, snake charmer to slippery, sly, fun but also menacing poems, born of precocious technical mastery and increasingly reckless imaginative abandon. Boyish wonder meets a cynical intelligence. Playfulness and seriousness blur to one and the same. In his best poems – and by now, the longevity of his 70s and 80s lyric masterpieces 'Wind and Tree', 'Mules', 'Why Brownlee Left', 'Cuba', 'The Sightseers' and 'Quoof' seem beyond sensible question – the rhyming panache and lexical grace lure you in. But so, too, do the brevity, the deceptive clarity, the eye-widening exactitude. Form and flawless execution jostle with a beady-eyed mischievousness and darkness, unpicking favoured discomfiting themes: death, disappearance, sex, divisions both personal and public, and the sense that our pursuit of meaning is, finally, a flawed and laughable quest, though not without reward.

One Thousand Things Worth Knowing is Muldoon's twelfth collection. It arrives midway through the poet's sixty-fourth year, a year following one that began with the passing of Seamus Heaney, champion to the wunderkind Muldoon, and from whom the once protégé now inherits the title of Ireland's greatest living poet. In truth, though, followers of Muldoon the pied piper have been pushing for his promotion for a while. When Stephen Knight called him "the most significant English-language poet born since the Second World War", echoing Tim Kendall's similar pronouncements, he sounded a degree of cautious deference to the old master, but the claim was clear. Even the most astute, punctilious critics have reached for superlatives in praising this *rara avis*: "among discriminating readers of new poetry, no one's stock is any higher," announced Michael Hofmann. The acclaim rings true. Muldoon really is as good as he seems.

Or rather, he was. Like one of his own hypnotic narrative poems, there are a couple of twists in the strange tale of Muldoon's fecund career. Since the early Noughties and the publication of his hefty *Poems 1968–1998*, Muldoon's work has usually been divided into two – what David Wheatley, with pious irreverence, labelled the 'Muldoon Old Testament' of *New Weather* (1973) to *Quoof* (1983), and the 'New Testament' of *Meeting the British* (1987) to *Hay* (1998). *Quoof* was arguably the high point of the early style, a book of pellucid yet complex lyric poems that conveyed both the tragic farce and violent horror of sectarian conflict during the Northern Irish Troubles, in a style as comically parodic as it was coolly matter-of-fact. It marked out the Postmodernist Muldoon from his more genteelly Modern predecessors, and gifted him passage to the US, specifically the ivory towers of Princeton. From there, the magic mushrooms first gathered in *Quoof* met the acid trip of 'Something Else Again', a mid-life mantra that exalted a poetics of wild connection-making, paving the way for the cultural stockpiling and myth-kitty raiding that finds its apogee in *Madoc: A Mystery* (1990) and *Hay*'s 'The Bangle (Slight Return)'. The former, a reimagining of Coleridge and Southey's thwarted ideal of an egalitarian utopia, is relayed from the perspective of a prisoner's failing vision (geddit?) in the futuristic city of Unitel, with sections often randomly captioned after philosophers. Are we to take such bustling extempore as an opportunity for rewarding exegesis, or is Muldoon just taking the mick, leaving us high and dry, as he has confessed before, "in some corner at a terrible party, where I've nipped out through the bathroom window"?

Paul Muldoon © Gerald Mangan 2015

Whatever your verdict, there's no denying such poems have earned an almost entirely academic audience. Schooled readers might think they're in on the joke, that the red herrings of allusions and etymological conjecture are worth the price of entry, but to me *Madoc* still looks like an overlong, winking yet all-too-literal illustration of the misguided search for "a moral for our times", one that a younger Muldoon roundly mocked in 'The Frog': "What if I put him to my head / and squeezed it out of him?"

Which brings us to what I'd like to suggest as the third age of Muldoon: the apocrypha to the two Testaments, which seems to bear the stylistic signature but far too little of the earlier understated brilliance, enough to make it suspect. In this often manic hall of mirrors where language and trivia run about, cartoon-like, to a soundtrack of canned laughter and the odd sentimental tune, things seem mainly to go from bad to worse, albeit by the perilously high standards of the Muldoon glory days. Starting with *Horse Latitudes* (2006) – though sparing at least the magnificent, witty, heartfelt 'Sillyhow Stride', a paean to Muldoon's mother and sister, and his musician friend Warren Zevon, all of whom battled with cancer – we arrive, via 2010's *Maggot*, at this new collection.

I've taken this review as opportunity for a detailed appraisal of the Muldoon back catalogue for three reasons. First, because I'd wager that anyone not wholly conversant with his poetry's trajectory would struggle to make head or tail of *One Thousand Things Worth Knowing*; second, because I honestly can't find anything like those earlier poems to amaze or admire in this new stuff; and third, because Paul Muldoon so rarely gets to any kind of point in this book I thought I'd briefly grant myself similar licence. The collection opens with 'Cuthbert and the Otters', a ten-page piece in memory of Seamus Heaney, originally commissioned by Durham Book Festival. Adopting the legend of the eponymous Northumbrian saint, whose famous piety and diligence afforded him a Doctor Dolittle-like rapport with God's creatures, Muldoon invokes some loose metaphorical comparisons with the late great poet. So far, so good. Until, that is, Muldoon's hyperactive mind, limitless love of arcana, and growing distaste for anything so memorable as argument or cohesion drown the whole thing out with, it seems, whatever popped into his head while writing:

The way to preserve a hide is not by working into it Irish moss or casein

but the very brains
of the very beast that was erstwhile so comfortable in its skin.
Irish monasticism may well derive from Egypt.
We don't discount the doings of the Desert Fox
any more than Lily Langtry's shenanigans with Prince
Louis of Battenberg. The 1920s vogue for sequins
began with Tutankhamen. Five wise virgins

– and so on (and on and on). If there is substance here – and surely there must be in an elegy for a departed mentor – the poem bombards you with so much disparate intellectual litter, you can't hope to sift through it all to find it. Some will say this lack of any point is the point, that confusion is king, but when it sets the scene for an entire book, and when Muldoon has been up to this sort of zaniness for at least a decade, it all becomes rather mundane and forgettable. "When I glance / from my hotel window," our poet observes, "even I discern / a possibility / I might too readily have spurned." Surely not. Still, there's always the trivia. Did you know that Roman women "let // their hair grow right down to their waists / for twisting into skeins" for catapults? What connects 'Barrage Balloons, Buck Alec, Bird Flu, and You'? "Arthritis is to psoriasis as Portugal is to ..."? "Wait. Isn't arthritis to psoriasis as Brazil is to Portugal?"

As Muldoon merrily loses his way in *One Thousand Things Worth Knowing*, in overblown tour de force after tour de force, letting his brilliant mind and unrivalled ability with rhyme, form and syntax too often overwhelm the hope of poetry occurring, there is the sense that the genuine alchemist of our times has become content to produce fool's gold. But then you can hardly blame him. Only one or two poets in any generation will ever know what it's like to be so gifted that technique, capacity and sheer panache come to implode on themselves. The epigraph to 'The Firing Squad' is an excerpt from a letter by Robert Frost, dated 1916, in which he confesses that "the poet in me died nearly ten years ago". Telling, you might think. There are many timeless Muldoon poems worth knowing, inside out and off by heart. But, for me, none of the like are in this volume.

Ben Wilkinson won the Northern Promise Award at the 2014 Northern Writers' Awards. He reviews for The Guardian and TLS.

PERSONAL GODS

Arundhathi Subramaniam, When God Is a Traveller, *Bloodaxe, £9.99*
ISBN 9781780371160
Pascale Petit, Fauverie, *Seren, £9.95*
ISBN 9781781721688

reviewed by Sarah Howe

. . .

The arresting title of Arundhathi Subramaniam's fourth collection, *When God Is a Traveller*, signals its connectedness to her previous book from Bloodaxe, *Where I Live* (2009), as well as its departures. These new poems are still concerned with a sense of place and belonging, but now accept unsettlement as the necessary condition of their spiritual quest. Interleaving the sensual with the sacred, they are drawn to the moments when gods and humans journey along the same paths, but might be barely aware of their fellow travellers. This nudge of intuition is beautifully described in one early poem, 'How Some Hindus Find Their Personal Gods':

> It's about learning to trust
> the tug
> that draws you to a shadowed alcove
> undisturbed

by footfall
and butter lamps,

The minor deity waiting there sounds like one who might be charitably disposed towards poets – "who looks / like he could understand / errors in translation, / blizzards on the screen, / gaps in memory, / lapses in attention" – as well as their readers.

These "gaps" and "lapses" work their way into the very texture of the poems, whose line lengths swell and contract in a way that feels both organic and necessary. More than in her earlier work, Subramaniam makes heavy use of line indents, scoring the poems and their nuanced pauses with her use of white space. Inviting us to leap across gaps of all kinds, the poet lays down recurring threads, sometimes widely separated across the collection, for attentive readers to tie up. And so that line, "It's about learning to trust", from the book's second poem, echoes once more in the title poem, which by no coincidence occupies penultimate place: "Trust the god..." / "Trust him..." runs the refrain beginning every stanza, less an order than a comforting hand on the pilgrim's shoulder.

Pattern and weaving become crucial metaphors in a collection that opens with a poem called 'Textile':

Some days
nothing in your wardrobe satisfies,
not the heat-maddened ikats, not the secular pastels.

The resist-dyeing process of knotting and dipping that lends ikat cloth its complex, multi-hued patterns subtly prepares for the book's last poem. 'Poems Matter' returns to the fabric metaphor, but this time in order to direct the eye towards the "air" in the weave, the "frayed edges". Unfortunately for a celebration of gaps and their power to imply, the concluding lines lurch into spelling out what is already understood: "poems matter / because they have holes". Indeed, this self-conscious *ars poetica* mode recurs just a tad too often across the book: Subramaniam might follow her own advice and "trust".

Several longer pieces take the form of multi-part sequences. In the numbered vignettes of 'Eight Poems for Shakuntala', an existing mythic cycle from the Hindu *Mahabharata* is piece-worked into a more discontinuous narrative. Despite the lack of footnotes, Subramaniam's reimagining brims with exuberant details that draw in the international reader. Sketched with a characteristic lightness of tone, the eponymous heroine is "just another mixed-up kid, / daughter of a sage / and celestial sex worker". Shakuntala's muddled origins and life of exile speak to the book's larger spiritual concerns: "What could you be / but halfway, / forever interim?" The answer is another question, "What else / but goddam / human?"

When God Is a Traveller is interested in how devotion, or *bhakti*, will emerge from the traffic of everyday life. Poems of mundane domesticity such as 'I Speak for Those with Orange Lunch Boxes' and 'The Dark Night of Kitchen Sinks' are some of the collection's most delightful. With its yoking of particular and abstract ("grease / and indignity", "foam and equanimity"), hendiadys is the latter's signature trope. It is emblematic of a wider movement, as the collection acts out its mingling of spiritual and sensual realms through language. Sometimes the play of clarity against mystery doesn't quite come off: "transfigured / by burnt dreamlight" ('You and I That Day in Florence'). At others, it channels the book's most startling observations: "our granaries lush / with words / and lovelessness" ('I Knew a Cat'). In such moments of daring, it is possible to see why many already consider Subramaniam one of India's most significant contemporary poets.

Pascale Petit's latest collection is no less attentive to the holes in the story's fabric, revolving around "the last days, after all he said / and didn't say" ('Emmanuel'). Her sixth and strongest book to date, *Fauverie* returns to the terrain of her second collection, *The Zoo Father*. The difference is one of literal rather than emotional geography, as the markets and cathedrals of her childhood Paris overtake the Amazonian jungle of Petit's earlier work. *Fauverie* is still preoccupied with wildness, but of a sort that runs up against bars.

The book takes its title from the big-cat house at the Jardin des Plantes zoo in Paris. Its arc charts the death of an ailing and difficult father – a man from whom the speaker has spent most of her life estranged. The poet finds alter egos for the predatory, charismatic, larger-than-life man among the inhabitants of the menagerie a few streets' walk from his Parisian sickbed. He, too, is caged, ferocious, "confined / to his bed. The plastic tube / that feeds him oxygen is his chain" ('Rue de Puits-qui-Parle'). A cast of big cats, including Teo the North China leopard, Black Ears the caracal and, above all, a black jaguar named Aramis, stalk through the poems. Held up against the amoral majesty of the big cats, the man and his violent history are transformed and even, at points, redeemed.

In its efforts to reconcile adult grief with half-remembered childhood suffering, *Fauverie* turns obsession itself into an object of enquiry: "All paths lead to the Fauverie / and this is where I come, again and again" ('Kissing a Jaguar'). One of the more subtle ways in which the poems connect is through their play with vibrant colour. The primal tones of 'Blue-and-Gold Macaw Feather', "lapis" one side, "sulphur" the other, invoke an object with two irreconcilable faces: a "blade" that could be used to stab or to apply paint. In such poems, Petit activates yet another layer to the book's title, recalling the artists mockingly dubbed '*les Fauves*', the 'wild beast' painters. Known for applying saturated areas of colour straight from the tube, they included Matisse among their number. Unlike their immediate predecessors the Impressionists, the Fauves no longer eschewed the use of black. Delineating through shadow, black works particularly hard in *Fauverie*, whether rendering the "solar eclipse" of a jaguar's coat ('Sleeping Black Jaguar"), or the father's corrupted insides: "your right lung, where it's // tar black, colour of a secret night / I can touch without gloves" ('Lungectomy').

Strung between trauma and survival, *Fauverie* is well versed in the art of speaking obliquely. Framed as a series of denials, the curious negative logic of 'Portrait of My Father as a Bird Fancier' evokes the structures of repressed memory:

> that's
> the father I choose, not the man
> who thrusts red-hot prongs in their eyes
> so their songs will carry for miles.

The speaker imagines a new father – one whose kindness to vulnerable creatures is beyond doubt. The poem draws its energy from the residual presence of cruelty and pain, even as they are repeatedly disavowed: "He is not the kind to tie their wings. No." The conceit returns in a later poem, 'How to Hand-Feed Sparrows', which offers the brutal man instruction in the art of gentleness. The daughter tells him how to hold his hand out flat for the birdseed: "the fingers bent back / so your palm is generous". The emotional push-and-pull of these lines, their psychological complexity, turns on that line break, in which the reader does a double take: the potential violence of "fingers bent back" resolves into something more benign, yet still shadowed by that hint of bullying pain.

One of the most horrifying poems is 'Pâté de Foie Gras', with its vision of caged rows of force-fed geese, "some with broken beaks, / torn throats, maggots in neck wounds". The way their necks recoil from the man who "stuffs the gavage in" is echoed – and flipped round – in a later poem, when "Papa feeds me scraps / I've coaxed out of him, my beak down his throat" ('Self-Portrait with King Vultures'). Such reversals of perspective turn on a pin from vengefulness to compassion, destabilising any settled power dynamic in the book's clinched embrace of parent and child, torturer and victim. They are among *Fauverie*'s most sophisticated and satisfying moments.

Sarah Howe's first collection, Loop of Jade, *is forthcoming from Chatto & Windus.*

WELL THEN

Rosemary Tonks, Bedouin of the London Evening: Collected Poems & Selected Prose, *edited by Neil Astley, Bloodaxe, £12*
ISBN 9781780372389

reviewed by Matthew Sweeney

. . .

Rosemary Tonks nearly got me killed. I was in the middle of the trawl for *Emergency Kit*, the anthology I was co-editing with Jo Shapcott. My friend John Hartley Williams had told me the poetry of Tonks was an absolute must. So I took myself to the Poetry Library at the South Bank and dared to twirl the wheel that allowed me to enter the shelves where I'd find the publications of the poets beginning with T. I was thumbing through *Iliad of Broken Sentences* when the shelves started closing in on me. I squawked, but the shelves kept coming. I can't remember what I had to do in order to escape with my life.

Two Tonks' poems made it into that anthology, the first in which her work had been included for twenty years (the *TLS* review of this book was inaccurate here, in claiming another anthology had rediscovered her first). Furthermore, lines of hers appeared in *Writing Poetry*, the book I wrote with Williams. In the chapter on 'Style' we quoted the beginning of 'Dressing Gown Olympian':

of a dead end, she replied that it could be a great deal more exciting. "I don't understand," she said, "why poets are quite ready to pick up trivialities, but are terrified of writing of passions."

Tonks found French nineteenth-century literature tremendously exciting and inspiring, and declared her direct literary forbears to be Baudelaire and Rimbaud. She spent a year living on her own in Paris, on the Île Saint-Louis, in 1952-3, and immersed herself in French literature and culture. But the world of her poems remained 1960s London. If I may quote Williams on this (as featured on the back cover) from his 1996 essay in *The Poetry Review*, "She wasn't just a poet of the sixties – she was a true poet of any era – but she has sent us strange messages from them, alive, fresh and surprising today... there is possibly no other poet who has caught with such haughty, self-ironising contempt, the loucheness of the period, or the anger it could touch off in brooding bystanders" (Vol 86, No. 4).

Not many women poets were published in Britain or anywhere in the early 60s, and Tonks was not essentially a supporter of the feminist strain in poetry. Included in the selected prose is a forensic and unsympathetic review of Adrienne Rich's *Diving Into the Wreck*. It's interesting to speculate whether Tonks and Plath ever met or read each other's work. Alvarez admired both, saying of Tonks that she had a "real talent of an edgy, bristling kind". There is some common ground in their work.

Another of Tonks's admirers was Philip Larkin, who put two of her poems in *The Oxford Book of Twentieth-Century English Verse*, one of them 'Farewell to Kurdistan', which late on has these lines:

> I shall go to the centre of Europe; gliding,
> As children skate on the diamond lid of the lake
> Never touching ground [...]

And ends like this:

> Life is large, large!
> ... I shall live off your loaf of shadows, London;
> I admit it at the last.

In the interview with Orr she says: "Although my poems are a bit dark in spirit at the moment, I want to show people the world is absolutely

> I insist on vegetating here
> In moth-eaten grandeur. Haven't I plotted
> Like a madman to get here? Well then.

These lines speak directly to the reader, which is one reason we chose them. Tonks brought this up in 'Note on *Notes on Cafés and Bedrooms*', the piece she wrote for the PBS *Bulletin*. Echoing Frost, she spoke about the need for "absolute freshness and authenticity in handling diction".

And a decisive emphasis on the spoken voice is heard in her work as a whole. She is happy to reflect on this in an interview with Peter Orr included in the Bloodaxe book: "Now I am trying to express the thought with a colloquial comment." Interestingly, she goes on to link herself with Cavafy, whose poems, she claims, are held together by the quality of the comment – "the comment of a delightfully wryly humoured man who has seen every kind and turn of human circumstance".

Trying to sum up the work more objectively, one could say it is fond of judgemental opinions, such as: "The English coast is more oafish than a ham." It also delights in contradictions: 'The Little Cardboard Suitcase' refers to "damned beloved women"; 'Addiction to an Old Mattress' ends with these lines:

> For this is not my life
> But theirs, that I am living.
> And I wolf, bolt, gulp it down, day after day.

And all the poems depicting affairs (some of the best in the book) suggest an ambivalence about the sexual act, simultaneously thrilling and shameful.

On a more basic level, the text is littered with exclamation marks, hyphenated words, italics, semi-colons and brackets. Not the usual tactics of the time, then. In Neil Astley's excellent introduction, there is a telling description by Geoffrey Godbert of Tonks attending a Group meeting at Edward Lucie-Smith's Chelsea house in the 1970s. "She immediately gave the impression of a coiled spring waiting and needing to be unsprung. Surrounded by the voices of conventional wisdom, she manifested the loner's stare into, and the need to speak of, the indescribable future before it was too late." It is easy to imagine the contempt she felt listening to the assembled gentlemen share enthusiasm for their cool, well-made quatrains. When Orr asked if she felt that contemporary poetry was a bit tremendous," thereby bringing out the contradiction at the heart of the work.

We are lucky this work has been rescued. These are terrific poems that will last a long time. Some commentators have tried to suggest that Tonks's stuff is immature. To me, that is like saying Keats's or Trakl's or indeed Plath's output is immature work. To cite Williams again: "Rosemary Tonks's imagery has a daring for which it's hard to find a parallel in British poetry." I will finish by quoting from the final poem in the book, 'A Few Sentences Away', which shows very clearly what she could do in a short space:

> My past, no older than an April night!
> A few streets away – boulevard scab of a hotel
> She lived in; her armchair voyages inside a bottle;
> Her pride, its great sciatic nerve ready at a word to –
>
> ...... England is darker than a thrush, tonight,
> Brown, trustworthy hours lie ahead. Suddenly
> My past hurls her dream towards me!
>   I steady myself.... but how tender, carnal, blasé it is.

The range of these lines, the staggering vocabulary, the jumps, the panache, the pathos! How many English poets of the second half of the twentieth century have risen to such complex heights?

Matthew Sweeney's Inquisition Lane *is forthcoming from Bloodaxe.*

BETWEEN THE WALLS

Ciaran Carson, From Elsewhere, *Gallery*, £11.50
ISBN 9781852356057
Antonella Anedda, Archipelago, *translated by Jamie McKendrick*
Bloodaxe, £12, ISBN 9781780371085

reviewed by Aingeal Clare

. . .

"The hunt is on / for this man / who runs alone through / labyrinths and ruins," writes Ciaran Carson in 'Poursuite: Pursuit', a translation from the work of Jean Follain. There have been plenty labyrinths and ruins in Carson's work, but none more dramatic than those of language itself. *First Language* (1993) featured the Tower of Babel on its cover: two decades later, the rescue job on its wreckage remains a work-in-progress. Nimrod, builder of the tower, turns up in Carson's version of Dante's *Inferno*, where he talks a Myles na gCopaleen-esque patois of Irish and Ulster-Scots: "Yin twa maghogani gazpaighp boke". Sergeant Fox in Flann O'Brien's *The Third Policeman* lives between the walls of a police station, and Carson can sometimes give the impression of living in the cracks between words. *First Language* begins with a poem in Irish, and Carson's excursions in French poetry have been extensive – versions of Rimbaud, Baudelaire and Mallarmé in *The Twelfth of Never*, the coaxing of Rimbaud's *Illuminations* from prose into verse in *In the Light Of*, uncollected translations from Francis Ponge, and now Jean Follain.

The format in *From Elsewhere* is that the verso page gives a version of a Follain poem, while on the recto is an original poem responding to the French. The verso titles are in French and English, though when 'Un soir se refait' becomes 'Reprise' one wonders where French ends and English begins. The doubling up in the title 'Contours: Contours' underlines this valet-like attentiveness, skimping on no supererogation. There is a serious point to these little games. In his *Inferno*, Carson has Virgil say "There's not much time to lose, so make it presto". As Matthew Reynolds has pointed out, the Italian word is not in Dante's original. By pressing it into service Carson gives his English text a chance to achieve an Italian dimension of its own. When we compare the paired poems in *From Elsewhere*, the convergence between French and English registers is unmistakable. Here is 'Sous le soleil: Under the Sun':

> A horseman advances
> his horse
> nostrils steaming
> goes from walk to trot
> over the blue ore
> leaves wither under the march of the clouds
> the cataract booms
> resounding fallout after fallout
> in the fields grey rabbits burrow
> under the sun everything appears
> a symbol of nothing

This stays fairly close to the French, with the exception of a little light embroidering in "the cataract booms / resounding fallout after fallout", where the French has "*on entend la chute d'eau / à grandes retombées*". The translator's embroidery becomes the fallout it describes. The rejection of symbolism pines for an escape into the sensual now, but Carson's response poem 'Run' detects unfinished business, describing a man on the run "from all that are after him / for what he has not done / in the underworld".

Follain's poems are full of this painterly immediacy, of "Indefatigable dazzling / terrestrial strangeness". There are also lots of Reverdy-ian doors and ruins, intolerable wrestles with words and meanings, and soldiers and butchers, too, for some reason. On the recto side of things, Carson's poems bristle with references to the Troubles, but suitably estranged or disguised, as though fed through the sensibility of a slightly removed observer – a mid-century French poet, perhaps! But echoes of the Troubles are only one part of the poems, and plenty of them exult in the visual sufficiency of the everyday, a seamstress "washing her hair / before a mirror / in a tin basin dented like the moon", "a child gurgling at a washing-line / of wind chimes made of old tin cans".

Carson meditates in his introduction on the different associations of basic nouns in different languages: English 'bread' is not French *pain* any more than 'wine' is *vin*. He calls on the oenological concept of *terroir*, which traces the wine's taste to the soil in which it grows. This is a less than universally accepted theory, but Carson's translations are certainly not school of *Blut und Boden*. Rather, they transport us to distant horizons. In his notes, Carson quotes a beautiful line from John Clare, who thought "that the world's end was at the edge of the horizon and that a day's journey was able to find it". The last poem here ends on a similar note: "A red insect trembles / from the green moss / between two flagstones / then begins to creep / towards / the unimaginable horizon".

A further aspect of translation and how it gets packaged for Anglophone consumption is the question of whose name goes on the cover. Follain's is not on the cover or the spine of *From Elsewhere*. Not so with Jamie McKendrick's translations of Antonella Anedda's *Archipelago*, where top billing is given to the Italian poet. The Tower of Babel features here, too, in an ekphrastic poem on Bosch's well-known painting ('Tell me whose house this is on fire...'). Roman by birth, Anedda often writes in the Sardinian dialect Logudorese. "*Bruciare, questo, non altro, è il mio significato*" ("to burn, nothing besides, is my whole meaning"), wrote Eugenio Montale, and that was all the way up in Liguria; the lyricism of Anedda's poems is even more sun-scorched and thirsty, especially when decked out in harshly consonantal Logudoric. "*Et sas nues, sas nues a sa thurpas fughint / iscanzellande dae chelu onzi zenias*," she writes in 'Limba' ('Tongue'), which McKendrick translates as "and the clouds, the clouds blindly race / obliterating from the skies / all trace of lineage". He writes enlighteningly in his introduction of Anedda's relationship to the Italian lyric tradition – her affinity with Russian poetry and sense of remove from the *continente*, as it's known, of the Italian mainland. Nevertheless, he has not resorted to any gimmicks to render this in English.

Another challenge for the translator turns up in a pair of Oulipian prose poems on the letters f and i: "f Is the letter of felicity", we read, McKendrick felicitously taking advantage of the similarity of the Italian *felicità*; more disorienting is reading "i Is the letter of hilarity" (*ilarità*), since, unless we're dropping our h's, it's not. There is a Pasternak book titled *My Sister Life*, but how does one translate that into languages where 'life' is a masculine noun? By mistranslating: My Brother Life. To translate faithfully one must mistranslate. These poems are full of bristling encounters between cultures and tongues (not least in 'Tongue' itself), and McKendrick points out how often Anedda uses *tregua* (truce) as a form of conflict-resolution.

Landscapes and lighting are often zones of conflict in Anedda's work. "I see from the darkness / as from the most radiant balcony," Anedda writes in a poem from *Nights of Western Peace*. Montale-readers may recall the figure leaning "*da questa finestra che non s'illumina*" ("from that window that does not light up") in '*Il Balcone*'. As in Montale, the play of light and dark can be well-nigh Caravaggio-esque. 'Between Now and Then: Accident' is a beautiful poem from the 2007 collection *Dal Balcone del Corpo* (From the Body's Balcony). It opposes a superabundance of visual detail with a puritanical desire to sweep it all away:

> Everything remained brimming with colour:
> lilac and cobalt and a grey-etched brown,
> only none of this of any use
> as retrospect might be. The wind
> without origin or odour. The hill
> a bare cone like Calvary.

The competing instincts assemble and disassemble the landscape before our eyes, before introducing an I-you dynamic in the closing lines, in a touch that is pure Montale: "The conditional was swallowed by the din. / I saw a few clouds tethered stationary in our veins. // You're going away, I told myself, already you're reading backwards."

Anedda's most recent collection is *Salva con Nome* (Save As), which is the Italian prompt for naming a computer document: save with a name. McKendrick's channelling of Italian poetry into English has long been invaluable, and in giving Anedda's work a name in English he has performed a hugely worthwhile salvage job.

Aingeal Clare has written for The Guardian, TLS *and* London Review of Books.

IN FLOODS

Martha Kapos, The Likeness, *Enitharmon, £9.99*
ISBN 9781907587399
Philip Fried, Interrogating Water and Other Poems, *Salmon, £10*
ISBN 9781908836625

reviewed by Carol Rumens

. . .

The work of these two American writers illustrates the enormously rich range of contemporary poetic practice. One treats visual perception in a slant twenty-first-century take on mimesis. The other foregrounds language to mount a resonant attack on Western politics.

Martha Kapos, long a UK resident, is steeped in the European art tradition, and has edited an important work on Impressionism. Some of the new poems emerge from a fascination with the visual phenomenon known as aerial perspective. As her endnote explains, this is "the term used for the way atmospheric conditions alter our perception of objects in the distance by causing them to lose colour and definition. Leonardo called it 'The Perspective of Disappearance'." The concept is doubly serviceable for Kapos, as it combines her interest in the nuances of sight and depiction with the elegiac lyric that has always seemed so profoundly to be her natural element. In this collection, elegy often comprises the search for an individual's likeness.

In the poem 'Aerial Perspective' the spokesperson seems torn between desire for the visible ("We're scanning the horizon to find your likeness") and a fear that things themselves may be endangered by being seen. Both the nearly dissolving, blue-on-blue hills and "that pointed village" (a graveyard?) are "at risk" from what she mysteriously terms "the veering edge" – perhaps alluding to the physical experience of driving away from a scene? The sequence of visual losses seems to be a release. The church clock-face "we can no longer read" is followed by the disappearance of the clock and the church "out of which only the emphasis of a face / is looking back hovering and oval // like the surface of a spoon / with nothing left to spoil the impression / of the endless things you might become." This perhaps gives utterance to what's conventionally described as the mourner's need to "let go" – like a lesson in grief befitting the post-Christian, post-Einsteinian universe of curved space-time and travelling particles.

Companion to this Impressionistic elegy, 'The Likeness' deciphers a specific face from "a mob of birds across a nacreous sky at night" and "a black satellite picture of Norfolk wearing / a necklace of sprinkled beads." Earlier in the poem, the "pale blue hills" reappear, and the 'Perspective of Disappearance' takes the form of the painterly but disturbing advice from "the ancient Chinese treatise" that "distant trees have no leaves / distant men have no eyes". As the vision sharpens, the lost beloved becomes intensely present to the excited speaker by means of two almost flirtatious lines by Marguerite Yourcenar: *"your hair, your hands, your smile evoke / someone I adore. Who? Yourself."* Even here, there's a sense that sight must be guarded, with necessary tactics to keep the encounter private, and distanced by quotation.

Kapos doesn't resist the representational: she simply plays with the focus. As her epigraph from Richard Wilbur says, "odd that a thing is most itself when likened". There's a poem, 'Venus', that begins with the star "Troubled, irregular / among clouds / the unfurling in the air / bright and bright", and proceeds by a series of vigorous, dark-bright, tangible similes (mooring-rope, forest cabin, lit window) for the invisible, salving emotion the star symbolises. Such delicate, fastidious lyrics surprise us continually into unexpected sight by their treatment of colour and line: "This colour will invent your last smile" ('The Invention'), "... as if sleep / round and white / held her in a bowl" ('At the Hour Sleep Loved Her'); "Drawn into itself / a word is a thin // shaft of vision" ('Starting Pistol'). Kapos's "likenesses" and images are fragile – though sometimes, I think, more

Cubist than Impressionist – but they also rediscover the everyday world, in all its mysterious familiarity, like the shape at the end of 'The Open Road' which "assembles itself into / your vague home."

Philip Fried's new collection blazes with wit and fury and impassioned warning. This is the poetry of direct political engagement, which received wisdom says is impossible to write, unless you're prepared to sacrifice the literary subtleties. But Fried operates with immense technical control and never falls into agitprop or hysteria. Confronting the many nightmares of "the security state" (expansionism, the death penalty, nuclear aggression, torture, rendition, propaganda), his poems avoid the first-person pronoun and the mimetic depictions of bloodshed or abuse, but use clashing registers of diction to infiltrate, expose or oppose each other. Sometimes, displacement creates a parodic effect: in the title poem, for example, instructions on how to perform a harmless electrolysis experiment "at home" overlap with the diction of a torturer's manual: "*Imagine you are interrogating water, / coercing the hydrogen and oxygen / to violate their bonds, give up each other...*" The instructions alternate with a denunciation of the enemy, water: "Foe of stability, / it erodes in drizzles, / revolts in tsunamis, riots / in floods and from covert puddles / takes part in uprisings." Like the 'how-to' paragraphs, the descriptions of water's subversive activity also insinuate a textbook undertone, and contribute to both the poem's grim humour and its grim authority.

Fried doesn't find his 'mixology' texts only in military manuals and gov-speak. The King James Bible spurs some of his most powerful effects ('On the Record', 'Canticles', 'Unnumbered Psalm'). Shock and awe are alive on the page, and chill the spine, in 'A New Doctrine'. This poem revises the Book of Revelations in an apocalyptic scenario, where "the rider called Faithful and True" annihilates "the Balaamites", by means of "tungsten projectiles, lobbed / From space, cratering at hypersonic speeds..." Realism splices the mythic vision, and rakes the comforting fiction out of the sci-fi:

A door was opened in heaven

And the four beasts had each of them six wings about him
And they were full of eyes within, thermal and radar
Sensors feeding data to systems controlling the trigger.

Nations broken to shivers

'Practical Mysticism' concerns the genesis and naming of the first nuclear bombs (Thin Man, Fat Man, Little Boy). Its soberly descriptive tercets begin like a creation-myth ("In dormant form, the fissile Godhead appeared") and conclude by detecting "our own image [was] mirrored deep in the formless". Other poems explore biological human processes in terms of geographical analogy: the spinal cord itself harbours "the fanatics of the body's homeland" in 'Homeland Security'. Delusion and aggression, "hubs of primitive faith and bloody vendettas", aren't imposed by gods and warlords: they're encoded in our biology.

Fried's poems demonstrate that whatever is made of language is open to contamination, morality included. As the soldiers in 'Moral Helmets' are advised, "coming soon is a Moral Positioning System / (MPS) to align your firefight decisions / With four or five of the major world religions". But, through their heightened awareness of the mendacity of words, the poems find authenticity, and document a vision of morality almost as a superior form of politics. The nuances of Wilfred Owen's 'Draft Preface' come to mind. "Yet these elegies are to this generation in no sense consolatory. They may be to the next. All a poet can do today is warn. That is why the true Poets must be truthful."

Carol Rumens's next collection, provisionally titled Animal People, is due from Seren in 2016.

SHAPELY BUTTOCKS

Angela Gardner, The Told World, *Shearsman, £8.95*
ISBN 9781848613713
Michael Laskey, Weighing the Present, *Smith/Doorstop, £9.95*
ISBN 9781910367032
Dan O'Brien, Scarsdale, *CB editions, £8.99*
ISBN 9781909585027

reviewed by Kate Bingham

. . .

Because the Welsh-Australian poet Angela Gardner is also an artist, and because she's chosen to put her own drawing, 'Out of Sight of Thought 5 (Tring)', on the front of this, her second collection, perhaps it's legitimate to judge *The Told World* by its cover: an image of scratched, unreadable manuscript lines with a charismatic tapir in the foreground like a snatch of prehistoric art on ice-scoured rock.

The poems are hard to read and charismatic, too, for as Gardner states on her website, she is drawn to complexity, "the disclosure of the history of mark-making and a layering of meaning" in all media:

> I am keenly aware of the distinction that locates experience within the body, or haptically within the body's physical range, and can therefore be anchored to the experience of tactile surface or of colour to field of vision.

Like this prose 'Artist's Statement', many of Gardner's poems start clearly enough. They're enacting their own complexity, of course: delicate, knowable, beautiful one moment, impenetrable the next. In the same poem, precisely evoked images collide with passages full of compound abstracts, regular punctuation gives way to control by line break, and lower-case line beginnings abruptly burst into capitals with the kind of freedom some readers might mistake for poor editing.

Not surprisingly, there is a lot of art in this book, beginning with 'History Painting', which explores the subjectivity and complicity of perception, proceeds via Sidney Nolan's Gallipoli series ('Ilium') and the Prado ('*Solo estoy mirando*'), and ends in the serene chiaroscuro of 'The Cool Shade':

> I drive into and out of each town through arcades
> of light and darkness
>
> Those long dry avenues of sun and shade,
> sun and shade. Sun
>
> and shade.

Gardner's use of motif (birds, skies, mirrors), juxtaposition (concrete/ abstract), and a kind of conceptual chiaroscuro as the lines dip in and out of meaning, makes it tempting to read her work here as a literal translation into language of visual art techniques. The effect can be dazzling. In 'Pollen', for instance, *waiting* becomes the wilt of flowers, their pollen a meteor trail, the trail a bone in an X-ray, the X-ray a line of poetry, itself uncertain and temporary.

Elsewhere, though, Gardner risks keeping her readers too much on the surface, not dazzled so much as blinded by the sophistication of her thought, and seems to forget that poems can't simply occupy the canvas-like dimensions of the page but must also unfold through time. Perhaps this is why so much of the strongest work in this collection is about journeys, which contain their own implicit narrative structure: 'Somewhere We Drive Through', 'Exit Wounds', 'How It Works', and the Keats-inspired eight-line 'When I Leave the Clouds', which, while sacrificing none of Gardner's complexity, remains intelligible in the moment of its wandering off.

. . .

Michael Laskey has been described as poetry's Alan Bennett, and just as Bennett's fans fondly look upon his autobiographical explorations as the ongoing adventures of a favourite uncle, so for Laskey's readers this fifth collection is a chance to catch up with Tim and Kay, the bicycle and the veg patch since we last tuned in.

There's been a suspected sighting of Japanese knotweed in the verge, but thankfully not much else has changed: Laskey's world still contains a post office, cricket fields, and reference books, all of which he continues to relish and probe in poems written with the effortless good taste that comes not just from wide reading, but from a kind of wide and generous living, too. They're short, conversational, and scrupulously unpretentious. In most, the relationship of poet to subject is the true subject. Many hinge around their middle line, unobtrusively arranged through symmetry of sound or focus, so it can't be an accident that at the collection's own mid-point there's a cluster of poems about words ("abacinate", "bayonet", "callipygian", "February"). This is the closest Laskey comes to anything as dry as theory, with the wittily playful ten-line 'Callipygian' defining itself as

> A thought I have often enough
> – it goes without saying – but not
> a word I'd ever use
> to express it [...]

> [...] too clever by half for me,
> calling attention to itself
> when I want language transparent,
> not obstructing our simply wonderful
> view of such shapely buttocks.

He likes to leave his readers something to unpack and the gift of this little poem, which disarms in so many ways, turns out to be nothing less than the secret of his own creative approach.

Like *Permission to Breathe* and *The Man Alone*, *Weighing the Present* is full of the dead, who for Laskey are both dead and alive in interesting ways, popping up unexpectedly in dreams and daylight sightings and even, in 'Deathtrap', in the poet's own muscle-memory, as "Leaning forward as I bike into town / this morning it's George Curtis / I become for a moment".

It's not that Laskey is morbid, he merely gives the dead the attention they, no more or less than a chopping board or desk-top stapler, seem to him to deserve. For many poets, of course, this quality of attention is an entry-level requirement, but few can feel so Englishly obliged by it as Laskey, who seems happy to acknowledge certain poems, 'Alternative' and 'Lap' for example, as a reward for services provided. In 'Visiting',

> though my mind's been elsewhere [...]
> eventually the flurries in the hedge
> get to me

and, giving his attention at last, he see not only fieldfares and redwings but also his place in their needful existence. As with all such gifts, bad things happen when it's abused, as the collection's pitiless opener, 'Not That He Wrote Poems', and 'A Moment of Hope' – another lingeringly horrific dream poem – show. Along with his inability to resist a pun, Laskey has always had a soft spot for grisly tales, but the harshness of these two poems feels urgent, directed against a self the poet seems more impatiently critical of than in earlier work.

. . .

The first book's out, but poet-playwright Dan O'Brien has not finished yet with the Canadian photo-journalist Paul Watson (a new poem based on their collaborations recently won the Troubadour International Poetry Competition) and this second collection, *Scarsdale*, shows he has not finished with war, either. The kind of war you can photograph makes no appearance, but the war that O'Brien paraphrases Camus saying "lives in each of us. In the loneliness and humiliation we all feel" is there on every page.

Scarsdale is about coming of age in a difficult family. A boy called Dan, who wants to be a poet, inherits loneliness from his mother and humiliation from his father. One of his too-many siblings is a suicide, and every poem a victory in Dan's own fight for survival. It's like a three-act drama: theme and tension are established in a long first childhood section, from which Dan escapes to Ireland to grow up in the middle, before returning – his own man now – for a showdown at the end. As often with three-act dramas, the strongest writing comes at the beginning, where the latent brutality of Dan's father and the primitive hatred the family directs at any and all outsiders, in poems such as 'The Dead End' and 'Raccoons', are powerfully articulated. By part three, some of this power has been lost. O'Brien renounces the violence embedded in his earlier language to show that the adult Dan is no longer a member of this particular tribe.

O'Brien is brilliant at pace. The poems in *War Reporter* hammer out their lines with hell-for-leather ten-syllable regularity. Here, equally skilful line breaks and minimal punctuation (very few poems have full-stopped line or section endings) keep the eye on the page and the mind's eye hungry for something to picture. These are not visual poems. O'Brien knows a good image when he makes one, but even a beauty like this, from 'Breaking the Ice', "That gold cube of light / in the kitchen overhead / with my family inside speaking", is written for the ear. *Scarsdale* is full of speech: reported, remembered, overheard, the speech of poet to self in the form of questions, and the non-verbal speech of poet to reader we call subtext. Written, one feels, to be read aloud, the power of these poems lies in the noisy physicality of their verbs. Escaping these, Dan's most precious moments of stillness are evoked through qualities of music and silence, as here in the collection's final poem, where he waits at night

> Until a student came
> whose footsteps were like a twin to mine:
> listening through the wall as he played
> over and over the same old song.
>
> ('The Music House')

Kate Bingham's third collection, Infragreen, is forthcoming from Seren in June.

HOME TURF

Alan Gillis, Scapegoat, *Gallery*, £10
ISBN 9781852356095
Paul Batchelor, The Love Darg, *Clutag Press*, £15
ISBN 9780957562615

reviewed by A.B. Jackson

. . .

Alan Gillis, born in Belfast but now teaching at the University of Edinburgh, is a prolific poet: this is his fourth collection in ten years. He now writes almost exclusively in rhyme, following in the Northern Irish tradition of Muldoon, Carson, and Mahon, and his poems are full of that region's vocabulary – sheughs, cacked, cowped, niddle-noddles, geg, spleets, breeks, glent, scroofy, scunged, sprootzy-dootzy (he might have made that one up), scutter, whang, whim-whams. His word-hoard is a veritable sweetie box, a binful of Dolly Mixtures; their sounds pop on the tongue like Creamola Foam. His attention ranges from urban dereliction to "sundews and fronds", his vision in 'Spring' is of cherry blossom and beer cans, the "here- / it-comes and there-it-goes of everything." He is an engaging guide, full of unflagging detail, full of blather:

> Get yourself outside to suck
> > up the calamity

> of hound-black howlers
> huffed up over the frazzled nerve-
>   ends of needle-furze,
> thrawn wheat, barley, maize, bulrush,
>   over the motion-sick
> surface of fast-frumpled reservoirs,
>   discomfuffled lakes,
> frothing loughs, scampering rivers
>   ('The Sweeping')

The cover blurb mentions Gillis's predilection for "hymns of praise" and "dream-like fantasias", and these elements are captured in poems such as 'Instagrammatic'. This meditation on a poor-quality photograph and our concept of the true-to-life could have ended after four stanzas on a satisfying note of closure – "We approximate one another. Then we're gone." – but instead, the poem gets its second wind and opens out into a joyous Song of Songs-style riff on his partner's body:

> ... your sense of humour is a ferret,
> your nose is a white-sided jackrabbit,
> the sweat on the curve of your neck is the dew on a tulip's calyx,
> your irises are the aurora borealis
> (and if these are windows to your soul, then you're a
>   chameleonic shimmering megaton
> of colliding electric particles blown by the sun)

Though we may accept the Rabelaisian good humour in all this, the fragmentation and fetishisation of women by male poets remains problematic; all the more reason to appreciate Jen Hadfield's appropriation of this same form in her recent poem 'The Ambition' ("My throat a maypole for eel-grass / My retinas red rags to bulls").

Gillis continually counterbalances the far-fetched with the down at heel, the unsentimental, the grit and grime of the actual. As tender and multi-layered as his own imaginative flights can be, he denies his characters the language of romance: on 'The Estate', we have "[t]ext sex, porno moans / in school corridors, / love rats on the floor / filming vajazzles on their phones"; in '21 Poinsettia Avenue', a telephone conversation between two women is interrupted when one of them is suddenly called to provide webcam sex ("Aye, a quickie. Still, it's silver in the hand"), while passengers on the 'No. 8' bus are imagined as being primarily concerned with "getting their hole". While the vigour of the language may suggest an air of gallus earthiness, there's a reductive aspect that becomes rather dispiriting after a while.

This book finally comes into its own with a number of poems rooted in Gillis's formative patch of Northern Ireland. In 'Before What Will Come After', a rhyming-couplet narrative about boyhood pranks contains less innocent elements: "guns in McGilligan's farm / somewhere, wrapped deep in turnip fields", and the character McCandless with eyes "darting, ready to target what they could". The story is picked up four poems later in 'Scapegoat', in which McCandless is hiding out after "a botched job" with the Ulster Freedom Fighters, and even here Gillis cannot resist a surreal diversion of mushroom-induced hallucinations – introducing, again, the question of what is real, what (or who) can be trusted. The location in both poems is Killynether, which also features in Gillis's first collection *Somebody, Somewhere* (2004). It is this touchstone of personal association, the *omphalos* of defining experience, that raises these poems above the trippy fantasias of Edinburgh academic life. That 2004 poem (titled simply 'Killynether') contains the line "At such times I curse my limited imagination", and this highlights the curious contradiction in Gillis's work: for all its wide-ranging expansiveness, its linguistic brio and energy, his subject matter is tethered to a rather narrow self-centre – there are no poems of history that don't relate to his own youth, and few poems of the present beyond his own nose. For a poet of such invention, such ability, and such productivity, it would be a pity if he didn't follow Carson, Muldoon and Mahon in venturing further afield.

The formal influence of Mahon can be felt in Paul Batchelor's *The Love Darg*, the follow-up to his first collection, *The Sinking Road*. The title is glossed in the notes: "A 'love darg' is unpaid work done for a charitable cause; it is also the title of a knitting competition in the *People's Friend* magazine." Readers of Geoffrey Hill will remember the word from *Mercian Hymns*: "my grandmother, whose childhood and prime womanhood were spent in the nailer's darg". Darg, then, is a day's work, and a word with particular currency in north-east England, where Batchelor's poems find their true subject. 'Love darg' is an apt term for the writing of poetry, too.

In the book's first section, Batchelor revisits his Northumbrian childhood: the mid-80s of Margaret Thatcher and miners' strikes. Family

114 The Poetry Review

conflicts are equally present, however, and the father of the household is an imposing presence in the opening poem, 'Brother Coal', written in subtly rhyming couplets. The environment is mapped out – terrace houses, "the rec, the tip" – and at the centre of life, both private and communal, is coal: "It stranged my mind that I could never lift / a shovelful or lug a sack – the heft! ... and yet a single piece / felt buoyant, quick and subtle, easily borne." Batchelor is also aware of the pitfalls of this subjectivity, this heavy nostalgia:

> Compacted sentiment, this pseudo-factual,
> homely, far-fetched stuff. O, Brother Coal,
> shine your torch on such complacency
> for shame! Shine your black torch that I may see
> each brush-off, cave-in and betrayal
> implicated in your comet's tail.

Memory is being mined, fragments are being fetched up to the surface. The tour de force of 'To a Halver' – a poem in praise of the half-brick – again draws together personal, political and industrial histories: the poet's father caught in a football riot in Glasgow; the Levellers fighting Cromwell; "the vanished kilns of Langley & Eldon". In its mock-heroic sweep and tone, it resembles Antony Rowland's great 'Pie' poem (and something of Sean O'Brien) but never loses sight of its serious, dissenting purpose: "history's ellipsis point, sign to which we must attend – / when words fail may you always be at hand". This section also includes a sestina on the subject of pit ponies, let above ground during a strike, and two finely balanced short-line poems about the death of a family matriarch.

The second section of the book contains 'The Seven Joys of Failure', a wry meditation on non-conformism in the face of galloping capitalism and societal snobbery. In 'Standing Male Nude' he examines the physical inheritance of the body, searching it for clues that might reveal the inner life or public role of the subject, the couplets again so subtly worked that it's not immediately obvious that this is a rhyming poem:

> He's not a worker, this one.
> He's a learned person.
> On those thin ankles he's
> top-heavy as a horse,

well watered and well fed
with all he can afford –
this room with its mini-bar,
Toblerone and small beer.

The physical focus and the rhyming couplets continue with a sonnet after
Baudelaire, 'Beauty', in which the statuesque features of the body are again
deflecting attention from the inner self: "Aren't I inscrutable? Like a sphinx
on my throne" – an invulnerable, supra-human construct that denies
emotion, and yet the thematic threads in this collection are so interwoven
that a counter-voice comes to mind from the earlier poem 'Returns', a
grown-up voice that disparages emotional display (in a child!) as "childish",
weak, unseemly. Beauty's bravado is not to be taken at face value; it invites
questions. The book ends with an intensely moving love song, albeit
entitled 'The Damned', a free translation from Dante's *Inferno*.

Special mention must be made of the physical book itself, beautifully
produced (as always) by Clutag Press, with three-hole stitch binding and
a wrap-around cover. The spatial positioning of each poem on the page
has been carefully considered and the typesetting is immaculate. At thirty-
four pages of poetry it is shorter than what is now considered a full
collection; with poems of this quality, however, these thirty-four pages
more than justify the cover price. For its impeccable use of form and its
unashamedly passionate engagement with private and public worlds, this
is one of the stand-out collections of 2014.

A.B. Jackson's second collection, The Wilderness Party, *will be published by Bloodaxe in
September 2015.*

LEVELS OF SCRUTINY

Miriam Gamble, Pirate Music, *Bloodaxe, £9.95*
ISBN 9781780371139
Lucy Tunstall, The Republic of the Husband, *Carcanet, £9.95*
ISBN 9781847772565

reviewed by Julia Bird

. . .

When visiting a small town, hours spent in the museum-cum-gallery are never wasted. Pore over the collections of taxidermy and beetles in boxes, take in the key local artworks, and you'll learn everything you need to know about the concerns of collectors and visitors alike. Miriam Gamble's *Pirate Music* is a mixed display of a similar sort, one prompting the reader to consider the roles of both animal and artist in the construction of a world view. The angsty 'Bower Bird' completes his life's work of arranging flowers and "glittering phenomena" to attract a mate just before he expires in a Shakespearean fit of fear of the heat of the sun; while in 'Bodies' (one of a number of horse poems) the process of breaking a horse – "learn to carry your weight / through your quarters, take a contact on the mouth / that's light but present" – is informed by the degree a citizen must or must not submit to society's demands. Gamble's animals embody her interests, but her artists articulate them. Or rather, they attempt to, but often fail. In 'Cuba', a diver says of a coral reef: "It is too perfect to describe, / and I do not want to learn / the language," wanting instead some experience to remain bubbling through the body and not be pinned down by words. In 'The Locked Room Mystery', art has died – "Let's admit it's come to a natural end. / The Golden Age [of crime fiction] is over" – yet we'll keep trying to revive it. The poem ends "And yet we still seek the impossible crime. / Listen. There's a house, surrounded by virgin snow ...". Put a fresh sheet in the typewriter, we'll give it another go.

Not every exhibit bears Gamble's level of scrutiny successfully, however. 'Dressing Fleas' springs from an Octavio Paz epigraph likening the artisan-made *objet* (as opposed to the mass-produced product) to the "difficult, exquisite and useless art of dressing fleas":

> a budding fashionista in the audience
> catches sight of their duds,
> and next year on the catwalks of Milan and London
> the look is brazenly passed off
> as the signature of the couture line
> at the brand new *House of Insect* [...]

This overloads the comparison. While 'Dressing Fleas' might be an example of a poem straining for effect, 'Blue Nude' (a collaboration with visual artist Douglas Hutton) is *about* that strain:

> Her lover is an island, far away.
> He writes of breasts
> tipped with raspberry fruit,
> of arms like alabaster,
> sends fat parcels
> to the poetry press.

The Blue Nude of the poem and the painting won't be defined, however hard she's stared at: "nudes are nothing – / form, structure, vessels for the roving self". *Pirate Music* is a collection light on the first-person voice. Gamble's own self roves through the galleries of objects and artefacts she's curated: you might find your self pinned up on display there, too.

"O remember the children of first marriages," exhorts the first line of Lucy Tunstall's debut collection, "For the seal of the misbegotten is on them." Who are these children? The poetic pixelation of their identities intrigues. Does the poet, in urging us to look to these "scene-shifters ... biders ... loners", introduce herself as such a child; or is she more concerned with the parental or step-parental perspective? No matter that this question is unanswerable: a major concern of the collection is now established. A family tree of poems follows, memorialising Aunt Jane, who "in 1956, or thereabouts ... fell in love with a beautiful / scholar from the subcontinent", and Great-great Uncle Charlie who piloted his traction engine along "a seam of moonlight on the river" "with nothing for the journey / but an onion and a piece of sharp cheese". So far, so familiar – but then, feel the ground shift. A sequence of poems, 'From the Pantechnicon', is an assemblage of found texts – newspaper clippings, messages from Buckingham Palace, wills, songs and letters – purporting to relate to the life of Barry J Gordon, identified previously as the poet's glamorous godfather. However, the notes say that the epigraph to the sequence – "Barry J Gordon, a beautiful young boy with extraordinary golden hair ..." – is "adapted" from a biography of an actual Australian art critic, sending this reader sliding down a Wikipedia rabbit hole to try to confirm Gordon's own biographical details. While confirmation is sought, the found texts assume a thrilling sort of instability. No longer the reliable archival record of one man's life, there's the possibility that the whole papery bundle is entirely made up ... and that opens up many satisfyingly pursuable questions about identity within a familial or historical context. 'Who are you?' this sequence asks. It answers, 'Well, that depends.'

Tunstall also hitches her enquiries to the horse. 'One Day a Herd of Wild Horses Came into the Garden and Looked at My Mother' is a humorous, tightly tethered account of an equine/human encounter, beginning with an affectless, one sentence per line description of a mother who can only react to the chaos in the flowerbeds by repeating, "this is extraordinary", before she comes in from the garden for a cigarette. 'The Random Nature of God' is, in contrast, a hands-knotted-in-the-mane, bareback affair. A herd of horses appears as if summoned by a transgressive act: "something in me, / in us, drew on the horses. Two years / of peaceful untroubled grazing ended / on our one night alone in that place." The language is clattering and threatening, trampling all over line endings and margins. This is a poet working with many moods, registers and identities – there's a sly surprise on her every page. Watch out for her hoof-prints on your lawn.

Julia Bird's most recent collection is Twenty-four Seven Blossom *(Salt, 2013).*

IN THE LIGHT OF SILENCE

Openwork: Poetry and Prose by André du Bouchet, *translated by Paul Auster and Hoyt Rogers, Yale, £16.99*
ISBN 0300197632

reviewed by Will Stone

. . .

In the post-war period, certain French poets sought, through the radicalising prism of the 60s, to authentically address the trauma of 1939-45. Among the most prominent was André du Bouchet, whose name is little known to English language readers. The neglect of Du Bouchet is perhaps not surprising, however, given the visibly unorthodox and therefore, to contemporary tastes, 'challenging' nature of his poetry. Entirely at odds with the ironical, self confessional, domestic or descriptive natural world preoccupations that make up most of published poetry today in the UK, Du Bouchet evades the linguistically embroidered confines of the outspoken self, and with the single-minded patience of a hunter seeking a mythical beast, shelters in the lee of silence, coaxing from the 'uninhabited' regions – that fertile loam of the space and the blank page – some mysterious residue of the spirit. This suspicion, this reticence, this reluctance to obey, unquestioningly, existing language, to celebrate a linguistic triumph too early, to recline on the linguistic chaise longue of complacency, constitutes the cornerstone of Du Bouchet's art. "Instead of creating words and sentences, I begin by imagining my silent connection to the world."

Du Bouchet's poetry is steeped in an emotionally charged awareness of landscape and the mute authority of the natural world. "Of the earth, I know nothing but the surface, I have embraced it." Du Bouchet, then, follows the now unfashionable Rilkean axiom of patience, the slow reaping of experience, where the desired poem is somewhere ahead but may never be reached. "I always write to make myself worthy of the poem which is not yet written. Without hope." But in evolving towards its possible emergence, the poet, stripped of illusions, and, significantly, expectation, may yet stumble on something that illuminates obliquely. It is not surprising to hear that Du Bouchet tended to eschew the fanfare and hierarchical posturing of the literary world, preferring to publish his work in smaller presses, and choosing in later years the seclusion of the isolated Drôme region of rural France.

While his fraternal contemporaries Yves Bonnefoy and Philippe Jaccottet have long received the attentions of literary translators here, Du Bouchet at least had a sleeping ace up his sleeve, for the celebrated writer Paul Auster was an early champion of the work. His seminal translations from the mid-70s form the stable core of *Openwork*, a handsomely bound bilingual collection that serves to reappraise Du Bouchet's contribution to twentieth-century European poetry.

Openwork takes its title from *L'ajour* (a collection from 1998), and includes a majority of poems never before translated into English. The book, which bears a portrait of Du Bouchet by Giacometti, an artist to whom he dedicated a number of inspired essays, is divided into three parts, constituting the early, mid and latter stages of the poet's oeuvre, with the early and late sections translated by Rogers. This sensitively curated collection, which crucially also includes poetic prose excerpts from the poet's notebooks, charts the evolution of a radical multicultural and trans-lingual innovator of language, a poet ever on the move, alert to any hint of stagnation.

Auster aside, the real dynamo behind this collection is co-translator Hoyt Rogers, whose irrepressible belief in his subject and oeuvre effervesces and glints diamond-like through his copious introduction and notes, leaving the reader in no doubt of their historic significance. Rogers is keen to show not only the French roots of Du Bouchet's poetry, but the importance of his second language, English, citing his acclaimed translations of Shakespeare, his versions of Emily Dickinson, John Donne and Gerard Manley Hopkins.

Auster as translator, fully immersed and well adjusted to his subject, ultimately proves a safe pair of hands. Though three decades presumably separate the translations, the Hoyt and Auster versions sit comfortably alongside each other, appearing to hand the baton on seamlessly. Although sometimes their respectful fidelity may seem a little too tentative in terms of creative freedom, their equivalents come with the valuable seal of consistency, as if they handle Du Bouchet's precious canvases with white gloves so as to avoid, like the poet himself, leaving any greasy fingerprint of impulsion.

André du Bouchet was born in 1924 into a cultivated bourgeois milieu, where multicultural connections were encouraged. He later remembered "an entire childhood with foreign languages being murmured in the background". Owing to family connections, the young Du Bouchet was exiled during the war to the US and this period of upheaval, the exposure to English and the sudden severance from France, crucially instigated in the poet what Hoyt Rogers terms a "dual consciousness". A series of life-changing shocks, commencing with the trauma of France's humiliation and defeat in May 1940, and the sudden absorption of the foreign, shaped the contours of Du Bouchet's poetry. Following these trials and travels, his early work, published in prominent American journals, took on an air of restlessness, of linguistic pluralism, his whole stance exuding motion and risk rather than safety, tradition and anchorage. His formative influences included the usual suspects: Baudelaire, Rimbaud, though surprisingly also Hugo and then further emancipation under the tutelage of Mallarmé. These titans were then refined by the example of principal 'mentors', the poets René Char and Pierre Reverdy. Paul Celan, the foremost German language poet of his time, as well as a multi-linguist and prodigious translator, was a friend and collaborator.

In 1966, Du Bouchet, along with Bonnefoy, Dupin and others, founded the influential journal *L'Éphémère*. Celan also later joined the editorial committee. Here Du Bouchet published many of his translations of English authors as well as those of Russian poets Tsvetaeva and Mandelstam, the latter with Celan's collaboration.

In the preface to 'The Uninhabited', written in Paris in 1973, Auster states:

The poetry of André du Bouchet stands, in the end, as an act of survival. Beginning with nothing and ending with nothing but the truth of its own struggle, Du Bouchet's work is the record of an obsessive, wholly ruthless attempt to gain access to the self.

And sensing the resistance that will come to Du Bouchet's stand, Auster adds "Du Bouchet's work however, will seem difficult to many readers approaching it for the first time. Stripped of metaphor, almost devoid of imagery and generated by a syntax of abrupt paratactic brevity, his poems have done away with nearly all the props that students of poetry look for".

But there is imagery. In a notebook entry dating from 1951, entitled 'The Piercing Thorns', such concerns are prose poeticised:

> Every poem is a ripped-off piece of bark that flays the senses. The poem has broken this casing, this wall, which atrophies the senses. For an instant we can grasp the earth, grasp reality. Then the open wound heals over. Everything goes deaf again, goes mute and blind.

In Part 1 of *Openwork*, Du Bouchet's philosophically inclined notes flaunt their energy and daring, leaping and flashing like so many salmon straining against the indifferent current. The sense of wonder at the natural world's resilience and dynamism and the poet's commitment to reflect it, despite the interventions of human folly, is encapsulated in a choice line from 'Here the light falls in step' (1955). "If the earth keeps breathing hard, we will wear ourselves out." His succinct lines at once impress and fox the reader with their odd switchbacks into obscurity, their false bottoms of meaning. Their improbable but gradually seductive rhythm serves as counterpoint to the conventional gluttony of unseasoned words.

In Part 2 we read 'From the Edge of the Scythe', translated by Auster:

> The mountain,
>   the earth drunk by the day, without
> the wall moving.

>   The mountain
>   like a fault in the breath

>   the body of the glacier.

And the glacier returns in 'The Light of the Blade':

This glacier that creaks

to utter
the cool of earth

without breathing.

Du Bouchet can also stun the reader with a single haunting line, left moored on the page like an existential marker buoy, as here in part IV of 'The White Motor':

I stop at the edge of my breath, as if beside a door, to listen to
its cry.

And here working the reader harder, in 'Accidents':

We will be washed of our face, like the air that crowns the wall.

In 'Late Poems', the blank page gradually overwhelms the remaining text, ushering in abstraction and a deeper silence like a series of fresh snowfalls. As one turns the pages, less and less language is visible; the spaces widen until only a few lines are left hanging across the page like wires in a winter landscape. But in Du Bouchet's eyes, this refining is inevitable, as he strives (like Celan in his later work, though with far less obscurity) to strip away the superfluous and edge nearer to the inexpressible. At the midpoint, even the wires give way and only one or two stump lines are visible as if the poetry is announcing its author's imminent departure. Page 263, for example, contains only the following, two-thirds of the way down. It is a fitting sign-off for the poet who, after a life labouring at the deepest seams of experience in language and art, implicitly understood the privilege of quiescence:

to leave then, like the snow.   without seeing

without sound.

Will Stone's Emile Verhaeren: Poems is published by Arc.

MIRROR-WITHIN-MIRROR

Michael Donaghy, Collected Poems, *Picador*, £14.99
ISBN 9780330456296
Don Paterson, Smith: A Reader's Guide to the Poetry
of Michael Donaghy, *Picador*, £9.99
ISBN 9781447281979

reviewed by Jack Underwood

. . .

*I'd like to be remembered for my poems, not my charming personality. I say
this not because I'm an especially reticent or private individual – but because
my work has a life of its own and, if it works, it's as much 'about' the reader's
life as about mine.* – Michael Donaghy

It's a decade after Michael Donaghy's death and the poet's "charming
personality" remains the biggest obstacle to developing a criticism of
his poems. While the work still "has a life of its own", the loss of Donaghy,
the man, described as one of poetry's "best-loved and most naturally gifted
practitioners", still dominates discussion. "When Michael Donaghy died
there was a carnival of mourning," writes Don Paterson in *Smith*, "...this
made the task of discussing Michael's work difficult, because all anyone
wanted to do was talk about Michael." Because of the outpouring of
feeling since his death in 2004 (both in bar-room anecdote and in print)

it's also been hard for readers who did not know Donaghy to approach the work outside of this context of a community still feeling 'robbed'. Donaghy's professed "ambivalence" about biographical readings of his poems should be enough to warrant a critical appraisal, led by the idea that they are "as much about the reader's life" as his own (it's probably – and ironically – what *he* would have wanted). But the best argument for revisiting Donaghy's output remains plainly that the poems, running off their own steam, are still good. Furthermore, Maddy Paxman's moving and profound memoir *The Great Below*, exploring her "journey into loss" following her husband, Donaghy's, death, should probably be viewed as an appropriately authoritative last word on the man himself. As Paterson acknowledges, "Few knew him well, and perhaps only Maddy Paxman had any real understanding of the complexity of his personality, or the number and tireless imagination of his demons." Meanwhile, the poems are still self-sufficiently working their "effortless gadgetry", and, apart from the occasional mortal prophecy hitting a nerve, they remain oblivious to their author's death.

Paterson's *Smith* selects fifty of Donaghy's "major poems" and follows each with a close reading. He introduces the book with "a plea" to "read each poem again following my comments", which is an exercise designed more to give the poem the last word, than to *bring-on-home* the quality of Paterson's insights. The self-awareness and sensitivity of Paterson's approach are commendable, and the way in which he problematises his critical position as a friend and editor of the poet is perhaps one of the most interesting aspects of the book:

> All this book will do is talk about fifty of his poems in an open-ended, unmethodical fashion... and, I hope, emphasise the various and multifaceted nature of Donaghy's work.

Paterson, concerned with how his tour guide's handling might draw scepticism, has clearly wrangled over what his book can actually offer:

> I suspect, too, that this is the closest I'll get to writing a 'how to read a poem'-type book; but because I don't think anyone really needs or wants such a thing, it's really just a book about the way *I* read poetry, or at least read Donaghy.

Presumably, Paterson feels that people do *want* a book about the way Don Paterson reads Michael Donaghy, otherwise he wouldn't have written one, but any vanity or presumption implied by this idea is rather trumped by Paterson's evident conviction or frustration that critical attention to Donaghy's poetry is thin on the ground and overdue. Despite his embedded position and the biases it might bring, he seems primarily keen to get the ball rolling:

> some may find this book uncomfortably personal and too dissonant with their idea of useful criticism... Donaghy's work will require a less improvisatory and conversational analysis than I've provided.

Behind these admissions is the sense that *Smith* is, in part, a labour of love, which, despite doubts about its "usefulness", Paterson nonetheless felt compelled to write; there's almost a nerdy glee about the close readings which carries an unexpected tenderness to the whole project. And anyway, whether a book is "needed" or "wanted" or not, is a pretty relative debate even for a poetry editor, so fair play to Paterson for instigating one within the first ten pages of *Smith*. It's not often you see a pre-emptive strike on allied positions as a first line of defence.

Readers "obsessed with trivia", or for whom Donaghy represents something of a master craftsman, the 'smith', will love the formal and intertextual aspects that Paterson unpacks: Fibonacci sequences, movie references, Renaissance art, the occult, the various rhyme schemes, structures and mechanics:

> There may be a great deal more mathematical intrigue embedded in this poem. There are various ways of arriving at the word count, but expanding $\sqrt{-1}$ [to 'the square root of minus one'] gives another 174 or 175 depending (significantly) on how you count the word 'devil-snare'.

Smith makes room for anecdote in its footnotes, whether it's the showman Donaghy outwitting hecklers, or the virtuoso bluffer, styling his way through a "half-hour conversation with Hughes on his *Shakespeare and the Goddess of Complete Being... too embarrassed to admit he hadn't read a word of it". And because *Smith* is very much Paterson on Donaghy, it predictably includes some recognisably Patersonian assertions for good measure: "all a poem *is* is a mnemonic aid made of words, whose primary aim is to get itself memorised". Is that all a poem *is*? What, *all* poems, just that?

Smith is an expert work: well researched, unpretentious, well written, and aware of its position as a starting pistol for further critical engagement, rather than an endstop. There is a friendship, a kindness (both 'in care' and 'in kind') about the readings, that shows Paterson admires and knows these poems so well that he could be writing about his own.

There will be some readers for whom the critical unpicking of Donaghy's "machinery of grace" will be less interesting. Paterson notes in 'The avant-garde', his discussion of the poem 'Hazards', that for Donaghy and his contemporaries there was a greater sense of tribalism between experimental Modernist poets and the so-called 'mainstream', but that this has dissolved over the last decade, "mainly owing to the wiser influence of a younger generation who just can't see or care what we were all fighting about". This dissolution, which has led to a broadening sense of "form", and therefore "craft", might make the fetishism of certain technical qualities in Donaghy's work feel a bit like someone explaining the benefits of power steering in the Mondeo; the idea that a poem might rhyme so well you barely notice comes across now as much as an example of unknowing camp, as it does a demonstration of artisanal prowess. Invisible formalism, I mean, woof! Clever boys!

Luckily, with Donaghy, camp is part of the routine. At a recent Paxman/Donaghy event at Goldsmiths College in London, Donaghy's friend, the poet Eva Salzman, quoted his piece on Bishop, 'The Exile's Accent', in which he acknowledges the influence of Auden: "that arch elegance, that courageous affectation... a somewhat campy note of displacement resolved by conspicuous technique, a mode defined by wit – in the Renaissance sense – irony, seduction, and playfulness allied with reserve". It's this "campy note" that sets Donaghy aside from those contemporaries whom one can still occasionally find earnestly aerobicising their iambs in macho displays of supposed subtlety and control. Donaghy's poems show off openly – ta-dah! "My people were magicians", says the speaker of 'The Excuse': the artifice, the *owning* of the stagecraft is part of the appeal.

Another of Donaghy's strengths is that he tends to keep the immediate subject of a poem, and the logic of its enquiries, open and clear. But this courteousness towards the reader is often offset with a slightly dubious, creepy, avuncular speaker whom you suspect might really be leading you astray. "Step in and look around... We only have to make them *look* like wax," says the weirdo, vaudeville proprietor of 'The Chamber of Errors'. Similarly, in Donaghy's love poems, the slick seducer is rarely charming, because his lines fall out too tidily, are too rhetorically well-oiled. But his wits are so quick and ideas so surprising, that you may end up feeling like you probably *would* anyway: "Darling, note how these two are alike / this harpsichord pavane by Purcell / and a racer's twelve-speed bike". Oh go on then, smart-arse. Just one drink, but I'm not promising anything.

Appropriately, *Smith* is published alongside a new Donaghy *Collected Poems*, introduced, as with the earlier 2009 edition, by Sean O'Brien. Served up on the shell, without Paterson's walk-throughs, the poems retain their puzzling depths, and the contrast between each of them is heightened. You almost have to pity the critic F. Olsen, who mistook Donaghy's variousness for a "fidgety affectation of style after style" (from 'My Report Card', *Strong Words*; originally 'Noted in Brief', in *Hieroplant*, 1993). While he was so often described as "Michael Donaghy: the Modern Metaphysical", almost like a sideshow tagline, the new *Collected Poems* gives a fuller account of his range. In 'Alas, Alice', lead by a logic seemingly produced by rhythm, you find each new image is a turn, like someone playing a game of patience:

> who dreamt blue snow and froze in dreaming and spoke by
> reading and read all evening and read by patterns blizzards
> drifting and dared by waiting and waited talking and called out
> once and called out twice and coughed grey clouds and carved
> four coffins

There's the surprising bricolage of 'Interviews', where transcripts of Son House discussing fellow bluesmen are cut and pasted into a strange elegiac narrative involving a woman called Yvette and her lover, who seems to be Marcel Duchamp: "Marcel makes a world around them, / A short, shining world." It's an odd and bold poem that would pique the interest of most of the experimental "ampersands" that Donaghy derided and feared would take over poetry.

There are the Marvell-esque (Marvellous?) love poems, and none is more carefully and tenderly poised than 'The Present': "Forget the here-and-now. We have no time / but this device of wantonness and wit." But while Donaghy "The Modern Metaphysical" is impressively equal to Marvell in what Eliot described as "a tough reasonableness beneath the slight lyric grace", the fact he could probably go ten rounds with Robert Browning as well surely means there's more to him than that. His dramatic monologues are top notch, whether it's the Renaissance-noir (Renoir?) thriller 'The Commission', the shaggy-dog pastoral-Classical 'Remembering Steps to Dances Learned Last Night', or his baffling masterpiece 'Black Ice and Rain'. Eliot accused Browning of exhibiting "too little seriousness" in his monologues, and the way Donaghy's speakers sidle up to you can feel a bit like he's taking the piss: "Hors d'oeuvres depress you, don't they? They do me." But by the end, again, he has you:

> Since then, each night contains all others,
> nested mirror-within-mirror, stretching back from then
> to here and now, this party, this room, this bed,
> where, in another life, we might have kissed.

It's a bit of a shame to see further poems presumably published from the "safe" and "safer" computer folders in which Donaghy saved his work in progress. The posthumous collection *Safest* seemed like a reasonable gathering of the work prepared, if not intended, for public viewing, and given Donaghy's famed fastidiousness and conviction when it came to editing, it's hard not to feel that, with some of these later drafts, you're rummaging through his sock drawer. None of the previously uncollected work really stops the show, so it's not a risk that really pays off, either. Finding *new things with each reading* is a cliché, and one that often mistakes the changeable nature of individual readers for fathomless depth in text (or perhaps those are the same thing?) but looking through *Shibboleth*, *Errata*, *Conjure* and *Safest* you're never short of discoveries. Finding new favourite lines or ideas is easy. O look, I just found another:

> 'Driving and writing have a lot in common,'
> he parleys, and we sit there, the two of us
> blinking into the average braking distance
> for 30mph, wondering what he means.

Jack Underwood's Happiness *will be published by Faber in July.*

THE NATIONAL POETRY COMPETITION 2014

Judges: Roddy Lumsden, Glyn Maxwell & Zoë Skoulding

The judges share comments below on the top three winners in the National Poetry Competition 2014 – Roger Philip Dennis, Joanne Key and Fran Lock. The poems are published for the first time in *TPR* and in the NPC anthology, which also contains the seven commended poems.

Roddy Lumsden on Roger Philip Dennis's 'Corkscrew Hill Photo'
'Corkscrew Hill Photo' caught my eye with its mix of naivety and complexity, engrossing sonic effects and fresh phrasing. I couldn't quite grasp what it was about, but in the best of ways – I wanted to reread and make my own story from what I was being offered. I couldn't place it geographically or timewise (does it jump backwards and forwards?), but that didn't matter. A stunning poem which mixes sweetness, sentiment, the visual and a touch of the grotesque, I'm glad we found it.

Zoë Skoulding on Joanne Key's 'The Day the Deer Came'
'The Day the Deer Came' imagines wilderness infiltrating the edges of the city and gradually reclaiming it. The first person plural is combined with a syntactical build-up to give a sense of collective anxiety rising until "all our sorries fell to the ground". Much of its haunting effect comes from the closing image, where the deer arrive with "hooves clanging / on the concrete like empty bells – mouths without tongues".

Glyn Maxwell on Fran Lock's 'Last Exit to Luton'
This poem had to overcome the fact I didn't know if it was a poem or a prose-poem or prose, and I wasn't sure it knew. Maybe it doesn't care. It goes swaggering through town like a vivid old-time circus, commandeering all five senses till they start to fuse with each other. It wallows in joy and rejoices in squalor, it makes the Now swell till it engulfs the before and after. It's Hope and Misery having a hot date, it's the one poem in a thousand that knows how to swear.

ROGER PHILIP DENNIS

Corkscrew Hill Photo

All afternoon she counts the sounds
until the fly-specked room crackles with silence.
Even the song thrush noteless. A thick drizzle
trickles rivulets down the window pane,
smears distance on fields, curtains-off hills
and greens the sagged thatch,
aches in the creaking gate and screws
watering eye to misting glass:
a hearse skids slowly up the muddy lane,
blurs in droplets on a spider-web,
spins sideways into darkness...

   ...rattling cough of cattle, rusty tractor,
   hinge of paint-peeled door, gears
   of cars forced to back in one-track lanes,
   buzz of pylons spanning the hum
   of outboards in the yachtsmen's creek,
   yelp of kids in the converted Mill,
   the soft click-click of a camera-shutter
   up Corkscrew Hill...

The casement steams with sunset. She picks herself
up off the floor, mouth dry as mourner's grin.
Her arm reaches, shakes, reaches again,
gathers the clattering jar from the shelf.

   "Cider?"
The landlord frowns, sniffing cat,
moth-ball, mould. She squares her back
on his fine view – the duck bob,
seagull clutter, gape of lime kiln.
   "And a nip of lovage,"

before he can point her
the off-licence hatch in the yard,
    "to keep out the damp!"
and smiles spittle.
Her flagon scrapes a scroll of varnish
the length of the bar's stripped pine,
past bleating townies, past the regular's chair
and the corner where the photographer
sits draining her valley
through a tilted lens.

Roger Philip Dennis won first prize in the National Poetry Competition 2014.

JOANNE KEY

The Day the Deer Came

*The suburbs dream of violence. Asleep in their drowsy villas, sheltered by
benevolent shopping malls, they wait patiently for the nightmares that will
wake them into a more passionate world.*

          – J.G. Ballard

Ivy ran wild in the airing cupboard; it filled our cavity
walls, absorbed our tap water and strangled our systems.

The boiler screamed like a speared pig. A wilderness nested
in the underground car park, the subway, as the wild things

came to claim our hollows, turn our dark spaces into arks,
our children into wolves. We woke to find beds not slept in

and scatterings of fur and teeth; Cinderella duvet covers
were clawed into quilts of blood and skin. We cringed at the sound

of antlers scraping and tapping on our windows; the heat
and steam rising from the rut in the summerhouse. All this.

It started with one small crack in the road; the wear and tear
of cars; the rush of traffic and baby buggies; the pounding

of feet and wheels; the slow soak-away. We ignored the scratching
of our skin and the rubbing of grooves – all the wearing down,

and through. We smiled at poppies secretly seeding our concrete
with the knotweed dreams that filtered into the sleepyheads

of our begonias, the bowling greens, our turf and garden magic.
In time, the fissure stretched itself wide and showed us the lining

of its empty purse, and as all our sorries fell to the ground, dancing
and spinning around like street performers, the deer came

without warning: heads held high and marching; hooves clanging
on the concrete like empty bells – mouths without tongues.

Joanne Key won second prize in the National Poetry Competition 2014.

FRAN LOCK

Last Exit to Luton

He's a *real man*, you can tell, all plushy skunk and a dog you'd do well
to avoid. Aaron's twenty-three; says he could wear my moony face
as a pendant, calls me *tweety-bird*. I hang around his neck and Aaron drives.
He's taking me out to get buzzed at a club. I'm wearing white denim, spotless
as a chorister, and we are sculling the druggy gale between the tyre shop
and the roundabout; we're leaving these scutty streets, with their pawned gold
and thawed meat, far behind us. We're away up the town, gone for the
    gavelled
abandon of *smashed out me 'ead*, for fighting *squib* with *binge*, and living
for the weekend.

Aaron is not like the boys at home, dimbulb chinless wonders who only
want to trap you in the maundering bondage of marriage like their mothers.
Aaron's got other ideas, got big ideas, and vodka, and jellies, and he
    understands.
I'm *mature*, need more than pliant writhing in a narrow bed that howls
like a chimney. He says *you're better than them*, and he's right. I refuse to
    end up
like that, like the girls at the camp, lank slags currying love and desperate
    quaking
from spousal apathy; to be one of life's pale remainders, scrubbing my sink
    and trudging
to church, burnt out on a soused downer again. I don't want to be tied to
    the site,
to the tribe, to the old men, their tournaments and sorceries; to a fist in the
    face. I am
special. I am rare. I want gilt and spree and perfect hair and endless fucking
    diamonds.

He will take me away, I know it. In the club we are spinning until my vision
breaks into dizzy splinters; his kisses determine directionality. I'm lipping
limoncello, lisping citronella, reeling round my handbag like a wasp around

a bin. I see myself in the mirrored ceiling, well impressed with the
    brittle shimmy
of me. Aaron is grinning, and I am watching the weaponised swag of my
    nails, rinsed
in warm red light and raving in front of my face, my own face, big as a
    billboard. All is
love, and there is God, shining like a migraine!

He *will* take me away, he says, but not today. Tonight it is back to his flat
by flickering inches, and then to bed, this mad cabbagey firmament, where I
am rummaged and squirreled by turns. Aaron is smoking, the smoke hangs
in the air like a spookhouse special effect. His back is baroque with spots,
a constelled mire. He does not tell me that he loves me, he tells me I am *old
for my age*, and I smile. I smile at his Jesus tattoo, pink and coy as a bearded
lady. Jesus is smiling too. I have no plans. I don't want to go home. I have
school in the morning. You know what they say about *gypsy girls*: our life
is either a circus or a zoo.

Fran Lock won third prize in the National Poetry Competition 2014.

CONTRIBUTORS

Simon Barraclough's *Sunspots* is forthcoming from Penned in the Margins •
Emily Berry's debut collection is *Dear Boy* (Faber, 2013) • **Paula Bohince** has
published two collections from Sarabande Books: *Incident at the Edge of Bayonet
Woods* (2008) and *The Children* (2012). She lives in Pennsylvania • **Traci
Brimhall** is the author of *Our Lady of the Ruins* (W.W. Norton, 2012) • **Tommye
Blount** graduated from Warren Wilson College's MFA Program and is a Cave
Canem fellow • **Gabrielle Calvocoressi** is the author of *The Last Time I Saw
Amelia Earhart* (2005) and *Apocalyptic Swing* (2009), both from Persea Books •
Natalie Diaz is the author of *When My Brother Was an Aztec* (Copper Canyon,
2012). She lives in the desert and works with the last speakers of Mojave •
Jonathan Edwards's first collection, *My Family and Other Superheroes* (Seren,
2014), won the Costa Poetry Award • **Steve Ely**'s first collection is *Oswald's Book
of Hours* (Smokestack, 2013) • **Annie Freud**'s third collection, *The Remains*, will
be published by Picador in June • **Knar Gavin** is working on a bicycle-generated
collection of poems • **Terrance Hayes**'s collections include *Lighthead* (Penguin,
2010), which won a National Book Award • **Dorothea Lasky** has published
three collections from Wave Books: *AWE* (2007), *Black Life* (2010) and
Thunderbird (2012) • **Sarah Lindsay**'s most recent book is *Debt to the Bone-
Eating Snotflower* (Copper Canyon, 2013) • **Fran Lock** won third prize in this
year's National Poetry Competition • **Pascale Petit**'s sixth collection is *Fauverie*
(Seren, 2014) • **Jacob Polley** has published three collections with Picador, most
recently *The Havocs* (2012) • **Claudia Rankine**'s *Citizen: An American Lyric*
(Graywolf/Penguin) was a finalist for the National Book Award in 2014 • **Eva
Salzman** is author of *Double Crossing: New & Selected Poems* (Bloodaxe, 2004)
and co-editor of *Women's Work: Modern Women Poets* (Seren, 2008) • **Stephen
Sandy**'s most recent collection is *Overlook* (LSU Press, 2010) • **David Sergeant**'s
Talk Like Galileo (2010) is published by Shearsman • **Solmaz Sharif** is currently
a Jones Lecturer in poetry at Stanford University • **Tom Sleigh** is the author of
nine books of poetry, including *Station Zed* published in January by Graywolf •
Danez Smith is the author of *[insert] boy* (YesYes Books, 2014) and is a Ruth
Lilly/Dorothy Sargent Rosenberg Fellow • **Greta Stoddart**'s third collection,
Alive Alive O, will be published by Bloodaxe in June • **Rosanna Warren**'s most
recent collection is *Ghost in a Red Hat* (W.W. Norton, 2011) • **Susan Wicks**'s
translations of Valerie Rouzeau, *Talking Vrouz*, won the Oxford-Weidenfeld Prize.
Her next collection is due from Bloodaxe in 2016 • **Dean Young**'s *Bender: New
and Selected Poems* was published by Copper Canyon in 2012 .

T. S. Eliot International Summer School

Senate House, London
11 - 19 July 2015

Poetry lovers and Eliot enthusiasts are invited to the seventh annual, week-long celebration of the life and writing of one of the greatest modern English poets. The programme features an opening lecture by **Craig Raine**, a poetry reading by **Sinéad Morrissey**, lectures, seminars, walking tours, and visits to **Little Gidding**, **Burnt Norton**, and **East Coker**.

Institute of English Studies
iesevents@sas.ac.uk | http://ies.sas.ac.uk
+44 (0)20 7862 8679

Manchester
Metropolitan
University

The Manchester Writing Competition

2015 Manchester Poetry and Fiction Prizes

First prize: £10,000*

Entry fee: £17.75

Deadline: 28 August 2015

Enter online or request a postal entry pack:

www.manchesterwritingcompetition.co.uk/ps

writingschool@mmu.ac.uk

+44 (0) 161 247 1787/1797

*Terms and conditions apply

Created by Poet Laureate Dame Carol Ann Duffy
and the Manchester Writing School at
Manchester Metropolitan University

Join **Jonathan Edwards, Fran Lock**
and **David Sergeant** for the launch of
The Poetry Review spring 2015 issue

Friday 24 April 2015
7-9pm. Readings from 7.30pm

At the London Review Bookshop
14 Bury Place, London WC1A 2JL
Nearest tube: Tottenham Ct Rd

Tickets are free but must be reserved in advance. E: marketing@poetrysociety.org.uk

THEPOETRYSOCIETY

THEPOETRYSOCIETY

**The Poetry Society and judges Julia Copus, Kei Miller and Grayson Perry
congratulate the following on being shortlisted for the Ted Hughes Award
for New Work in Poetry 2014**

Carrie Etter *Imagined Sons*
Patience Agbabi *Telling Tales*
Imtiaz Dharker *Over the Moon*
Andrew Motion *Coming Home*
Alice Oswald *Tithonus*

The winner will be announced at the awards
event in London on 2 April 2015. For more
information, visit www.poetrysociety.org.uk

**TED HUGHES
AWARD FOR
NEW WORK
IN POETRY**

Crow by Leonard Baskin. Reproduced by kind permission
of Lisa Baskin and the Estate of Leonard Baskin.

LEDBURY POETRY FESTIVAL
3-12 JULY 2015

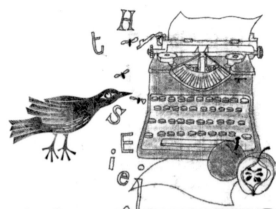

POETRY COMPETITION
JUDGE: DERYN REES-JONES

Deryn Rees-Jones's most recent books are *And You, Helen* with Charlotte Hodes (Seren, 2014) and *Burying the Wren* (2012) shortlisted for the Roland Mathias and T.S. Eliot Prize. She teaches literature at the University of Liverpool and is the new editor of Pavilion Poetry.

First Prize: £1000 cash and a course at Tŷ Newydd, The National Writers' Centre for Wales.
www.tynewydd.org

Second Prize: £250

Third Prize: £100

All winners get to read at the 2016 Festival – if abroad there is the possibility of Skyping at the winners' event.

For the first time this year to make it easier (particularly for our international poets) you can enter and pay online via Paypal. There is an additional 0.75p charge for this service.

Check the rules of entry at
www.poetry-festival.co.uk/poetry-competition.html

Follow us on Twitter
@ledburyfest
or find us on Facebook
poetry-festival.co.uk

Canolfan
Ysgrifennu
Tŷ Newydd
Writers' Centre

Supported using public funding by
ARTS COUNCIL ENGLAND

Creative writing
courses and retreats

ARVON

"These are
life-enhancing
weeks"
—*Simon Armitage*

arvon.org

**Fiction, Poetry, Non-Fiction
& Life Writing, Theatre, Film,
TV, Radio, Writing For Children**

MA in Writing Poetry

A ground-breaking collaboration between Newcastle University and the Poetry School: a new Masters degree in Writing Poetry*.

- Two years part time
- Starting September 2015
- Firmly rooted in the publishing, performing and promoting poetry world
- Competitively priced: £2,750 per year
- Unique combination of small group and individual teaching
- Study in Newcastle or London
- Newcastle tutors include Sean O'Brien and W N Herbert
- Newcastle teaching centre - full student amenities, access to Newcastle Centre of Literary Arts' event programme
- London tutors: Roddy Lumsden and Clare Pollard
- London teaching centre - close to Saison Poetry Library and other central London cultural hubs, at the heart of a thriving poetry community
- Newcastle and London students come together for an annual joint Summer School
- MA features guest tutors from the Poetry School's established teaching community

*Subject to the full Newcastle University approval process.

Applications will open later this year - to register your interest, please email Joanne Brandon at **coordinator@poetryschool.com** (for study in London) or Melanie Birch at **Melanie.Birch@newcastle.ac.uk** (for study in Newcastle).